THE
INDIA
SERIES

The **India Series** introduces the rich and
vibrant experience that is India through a
documentation of its myriad aspects – from
art to architecture, history, destinations,
people and the environment.

Authoritative, lavishly illustrated and written
in an accessible and lively style, each book
focuses on a unique aspect of India, revealing
an exciting new world and providing a
stepping-stone to future discovery.

The Harmony Furnishing product line from the textile division of Reliance Industries Limited, ably guided by Mrs Tina Anil Ambani, has been a patron of art and culture for many years. It has supported the establishment of the Site Museum at Elephanta caves and has taken various initiatives including art auctions to augment funds, supporting community development programmes for the benefit of the people of the island.

The publisher gratefully acknowledges the support of
Harmony Furnishing, Reliance Industries Limited (Textile Division)

ELEPHANTA

The publisher gratefully acknowledges the support of
Indian National Trust for Art and Cultural Heritage (INTACH), Mumbai

ELEPHANTA

GEORGE MICHELL

PHOTOGRAPHY   BHARATH RAMAMRUTHAM

INDIA BOOK HOUSE PVT LTD

CONTENTS

Preface

The man-made caves on Elephanta island in Mumbai harbour attract hundreds of visitors each day. Most come to marvel at the magnificent sculptures of Shiva, the greatest of all Hindu gods, carved onto the walls inside the main cave. Though created more than fourteen hundred years ago and now badly damaged by time, weather and countless acts of vandalism, the sculptures here still communicate the power of the god. For this is the home of Shiva, the place where he displays his paradoxical and mysterious nature.

A view of the island of Elephanta.

A trip to Elephanta is always appealing, since it involves a withdrawal from the distractions and disturbances of Mumbai. Several journeys have to be undertaken in order to reach the caves: water must be crossed, a mountain climbed and a cave entered. For many people, this passage across, upward and inward is more than a mere excursion; it is a progression towards the world of the god, a pilgrimage to Shiva's temple. Even for those unfamiliar with the myths visualised here so forcefully in stone, the sculptures can be appreciated for their outstanding artistic qualities. Indeed, they are among the greatest masterpieces of Hindu art in its first formative phase of development that lasted from the 4th to the 9th century AD.

Elephanta has been the subject of innumerable reports and studies, however, the caves remain enigmatic. Virtually nothing is known about

The main cave at Elephanta as it appeared in the early 19th century.

who was responsible for creating them or when they were excavated, nor is there any firm historical foundation for the popular spiritual interpretations of the sculptures. Yet it is not difficult to recognise the ethical and didactic underpinnings of classical Hindu philosophy in these magnificent works of art. Hence their enduring fascination.

MAIN CAVE

The north entrance to the main cave as it appeared in the 19th century.

THE ISLAND OF ELEPHANTA is situated about 11 km northwest of Apollo
Bunder, the departure point for the ferries to the caves. The island consists
of two hills separated by a narrow valley, gradually rising to the east until it
reaches a height of almost 200 m above the sea. For most of its area, this
island is thickly wooded with palm, mango, tamarind, *karaunda* and other
trees; its 7 km of coastline is fringed with sprawling mangroves. These trees
and bushes give an idea of the luxuriant vegetation of the Mumbai area
before the development of the city. As for the rocky fabric of the island
itself, this is a form of basalt known as trap.

About twelve hundred people inhabit three small villages on Elephanta island. Their chief occupations are fishing, growing rice, rearing a few animals, and repairing and cleaning boats; the tourist trade also provides many locals with work in the growing numbers of small restaurants and shops. For these inhabitants, the island has always been known as Gharapuri, or simply Puri. The present name of Elephanta actually derives from a colossal basalt statue of an elephant (see page 2) measuring about 4.5 m long by 2.4 m high, which once stood near Raj Bunder, the old landing place near the southern point of the island, where most people arrived in the past. In the course of the 19th century, this statue began to disintegrate and the stone fragments were removed to Victoria Gardens, now called Veermata Jijabai Bhonsle Udyan, where they were reset. The reconstructed elephant can still be seen here (see page 93).

Ferries running to Elephanta now land at a new jetty, some distance away from Raj Bunder, on the northern shore of the island. A short walk along the jetty leads to a flight of steps which ascends to the caves. The climb ends at the main cave on the side of the western hill of the island at an elevation of about 85 m above sea level. After the ticket counter opposite the new site museum is a paved open terrace shaded by large neem trees, from which there is a fine view to the northeast, with a distant prospect of the water below. The entrance to the cave, which lies to the south, is a man-made opening framed by architectural pillars and pilasters. Rocky cliffs fringed by trees rise above and to either side; a cleft to the left leads to an open court through which the cave may also be entered.

Though the main cave is the principal attraction at Elephanta, there are other rock-cut monuments on the island (see pages 90-91). Worship no longer takes place in any of these excavated sanctuaries, which have been accorded the status of monuments under the care of the Archaeological Survey of India. Even so, local inhabitants of Elephanta and occasional pilgrims do offer flowers to the *linga*, the phallic emblem of the god Shiva, installed within the main cave. At the Shivaratri festival celebrated in late January or early February, the island receives a large number of people, many of whom come to pay their respects to Shiva, who is also known as Mahadeva and Maheshvara. On such occasions, the cave functions once again as a place of worship crowded with devotees.

ARCHITECTURE

The triple-bayed entrance, which is seen first on reaching the main cave at Elephanta, gives little idea of the interior space that lies beyond, artificially excavated into the basalt fabric of the mountain. The cave interior is laid out as a great columned hall, approximately 42.5 m deep, lit by entrances on three sides. It is divided into bays by rows of free-standing columns, with

additional half-columns set into the walls. These columns define a plan of five by five bays, with triple-bayed extensions on the north, east and west. These lead to open entrances that permit light to flow into the depths of the interior from three sides. While the north entrance is approached directly from the paved court across which most people pass, the entrances on the east and west give access to artificially excavated courts within the fabric of the hill that are open to the sky.

The cave's architectural elements are mainly restricted to columns, brackets and beams, which give the appearance of being structural features even though they are actually monolithic, having been cut out of the rock. The free-standing columns and half-columns set into the walls are all of the same type, with the lower shafts taking a plain cubical form and the upper shafts being circular and fluted; the transition is marked by miniature squatting *ganas*, or dwarfs, which are carved at the corners. The columns are topped by circular compressed-cushion capitals that continue the concave flutings of the shafts beneath. The brackets, which have rolled sides, are linked together by shallow beams that run along the

East portico of the main cave (facing page), *possibly the original entrance. North portico* (top) *through which the cave is now entered. Columned interior of the cave* (centre). *Fluted shafts and circular compressed-cushion capitals of the columns* (right).

cave ceiling. Since neither the floor nor the ceiling are perfectly horizontal, the overall height of the columns, brackets and beams varies from about 4.9 m to 5.6 m. Today the cave interior presents a complete set of columns, but quite a few are partly modern reconstructions; the old engravings and photographs show many broken columns and brackets lying in pieces in the pools of water with which the cave interior was often filled (see pages 110-111). The only other architectural feature of interest within the cave is the square shrine accommodating the Shiva *linga*, occupying one of the bays. The shrine presents plain walls with doorways in the middle of four

sides approached by steps and flanked by large *dvarapalas*, or guardian figures. Inside the chamber is the *linga* standing on a pedestal more than 3 metres square; the *linga* itself rises to a height of one metre. Like the columns of the interior, the shrine walls, doorways and the pedestal are all monolithic; the *linga*, however, is fashioned from a separate block of stone.

All these features serve as a setting for a magnificent series of sculpture panels carved into the walls of the interior of the cave, on either side of the entrances on the north, east and west, and in the three bays along the rear (south) wall. These panels occupy most of the full wall spaces of a single bay of the plan, measuring some 3.5 m to 4 m wide and about 3.7 m to 4 m high; they are framed by half-columns on either side, aligned with the free-standing columns of the hall. The panels take the form of deeply-cut compositions recessed up to 2 m into the walls. Since the carvings wrap around three sides of this scooped out space, the overall composition takes on an almost three-dimensional quality. As for the other walls within the cave, these are altogether plain and massive, as is the ceiling, thereby contrasting with the deeply-cut sculptures. (For the overall distribution of these architectural elements and the wall sculptures, see pages 24-25.)

View along the east-west axis of the main cave interior towards the **linga** *shrine (preceding pages). Sadashiva or Eternal Shiva panel (facing page), recessed into the rear wall of the cave, at the end of the north-south axis. Detail of the central head of Sadashiva (above).*

PLAN

As can be seen from Figure 1, the interior of the main cave at Elephanta has an overall geometric configuration. The slight irregularities responsible for the lack of full spatial perfection were doubtless caused by the difficulties in excavating into rock, since the interior space had to be created by removing stone rather than adding exterior walls. That a geometric regularity was intended can be assumed from the symmetrical layout of the plan, which is laid out as a square of five by five smaller square bays, with triple-bayed extensions on four sides, each bay measuring about 5.5 metres square. The actual positions of the free-standing and engaged columns are determined by the corners of these bays, which create a complicated but symmetrically stepped outline with 12 corners. Triple rows of seven bays and double rows of five and three bays running in both directions, give a total of 37 bays. Since one of these bays to the west of the central point of the hall is

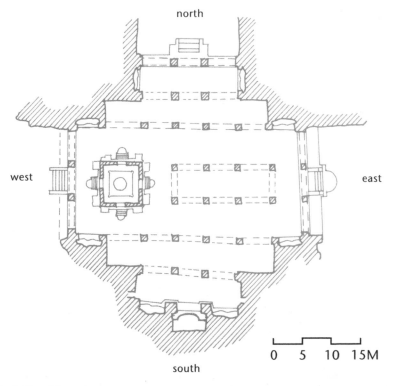

Figure 1: Plan of the main cave.

occupied by the *linga* sanctuary, the total number of open bays is reduced to 36 (see Figure 2). This numerical scheme corresponds to the mandalas, or symbolic diagrams representing the universe, which regulate the plans of Hindu temples and have an essential role to play in their sacred architecture. Mandala plans are symmetrically and mathematically conceived, being generally based on 9, 16 or 25 squares. At the Elephanta main cave there is a total of 36 squares, an equally auspicious number for a Hindu temple.

This mandala plan of 36 bays is complemented by two intersecting axes running through the middle of the cave, aligned with the cardinal points (see Figure 3). One axis links the two entrances positioned in the middle of the eastern and western triple-bayed extensions, upon which is positioned the *linga* within the sanctuary; another axis runs from the entrance in the triple-bayed extension on the north to the sculptural composition located in the corresponding position on the south. This last point is marked by the magnificent triple-headed bust of Shiva, here referred to as Sadashiva or

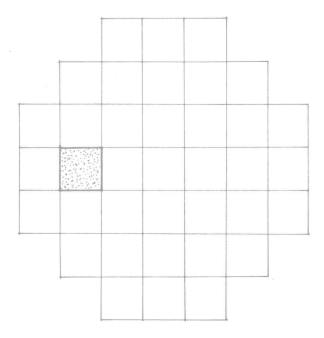

Figure 2: Layout of the plan in squares; the dotted square is occupied by the linga *shrine, the other 36 squares comprise the columned hall of the main cave.*

Eternal Shiva, deeply set into the middle of the rear (south) wall of the cave. Movement along these two axes offers quite different experiences: the east-west axis leads to the *linga* sanctuary where Shiva is worshipped in a symbolic, non-figural form, while the north-south axis culminates in a majestic triple-headed figural representation of the god.

The *linga* sanctuary and the Sadashiva panel are related spatially to form part of the overall geometry of the plan. If their actual positions within the cave are plotted on the two axes running through the interior, it will be seen that they are mathematically related, Sadashiva being located at double the distance from the central point of the cave than the *linga* itself. This configuration leads to a combination of two axes and two circles, the latter with diameters of about 22 m and 44 m; that is, in a proportion of 1:2 (see Figure 4). This geometric scheme not only determines the precise locations of the two most ritually significant elements of the cave, it also contributes to the mathematical complexity of the plan.

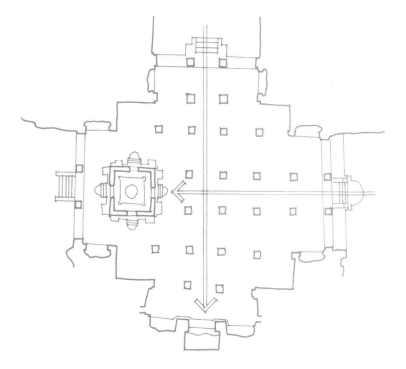

Figure 3: The east-west axis leading to the **linga** *shrine, and the north-south axis culminating in the impressive triple-headed bust of Sadashiva together form the double-axial scheme of the cave interior.*

Yet further relationships may be discovered when the squares, circles and axes are combined (see Figures 5 and 6). In these reconstructions of the original geometric conception dominating the cave's interior, the furthest points of the plan, where the axes and outer circle meet, are marked by specific architectural elements: the flights of access steps outside the entrances on the north, east and west, and the rear wall of the recess that accommodates Sadashiva. Such a scheme combines the static mathematical perfection of a mandala with the dynamics of a double axial system of movement, thereby creating a unique and complex plan intended to serve the rituals of worship for which the cave was intended.

Figure 4: The two circles in combination with the two axes, determine the position of the linga *shrine and Sadashiva.*

Figure 5: The relationship of circles and squares underlying the plan, creates a mandala-like diagram.

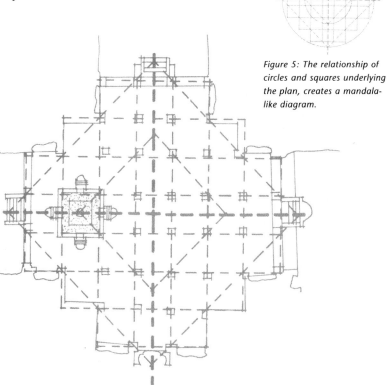

Figure 6: Squares and axes superimposed on the plan.

Shiva as Lord of Yogis,
Yogishvara

Shiva Impaling Andhaka,
Andhakasuravadha

Shiva Dancing

NORTH
ENTRANCE

WEST
COURT

Linga Shrine

Shiva Dancing

Marriage of Shiva and
Parvati, Kalyanasundara

Shiva Bearing Ganga,
Gangadhara

Eternal Shiva, Sadashiva

PLAN OF THE
MAIN CAVE
LOCATING THE
MAJOR
SCULPTURE
COMPOSITIONS

va as Lord of Yogis, Yogishvara

Ravana Lifting Mount Kailasa

N

EAST
COURT

*Shiva Gambling with Parvati,
Umamaheshvara*

Karttikeya

Guardian Figure, Dvarapala

*va as the Androgyne,
hanarishvara*

Mother Goddesses, Matrikas

SCULPTURE

Having considered the mathematical and geometric components of the plan of the main cave, it is now necessary to examine the sculpture panels of the interior. These are arranged in four related sets: three pairs just inside the north, east and west entrances to the cave, and a trio cut into the rear (south) wall (see Figure 7). While these panels will be separately dealt with in greater detail later, it is appropriate here to survey the overall stylistic characteristics that may still be appreciated in spite of the incomplete and damaged state of the sculptures.

Except for the Sadashiva, all of the panels focus on a central larger figure of Shiva surrounded by a crowd of smaller and lesser consorts, attendants,

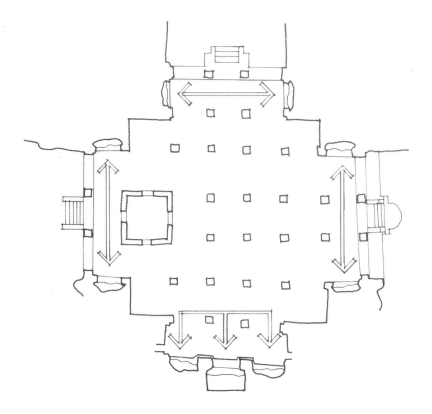

Figure 7 (above): *The four related groups of sculptures dominating the cave interior. The damaged guardian figure* (facing page) *beside the north doorway of the* linga *shrine.*

Central head of Sadashiva, showing Shiva in a calm and reflective mood.

celestials and other beings. The god is represented with a fully rounded, somewhat cylindrical torso and limbs, swaying slightly to one side, the head often held at a different angle to that of the body. The facial expression is invariably calm and reflective, an effect achieved by the lowered eyelids;

Shiva in a vengeful form while impaling the demon Andhaka.

the same is true for the central head of Sadashiva. As for the left head of
Sadashiva and that of Shiva impaling Andhaka, it is the demonic aspect
of the god that is emphasised; hence the curling eyebrows, glaring eyes and
open mouth with protruding tusks. In most other depictions of the god, the

smooth modelling of the face, with flattish cheeks, broad nose and fleshy lips, contrasts with the richly detailed treatment of the crown and headdress with *jatas*, or matted locks, some of which fall down onto one shoulder. Shiva is generally dressed simply with a thread running down over his chest; yet he is adorned with elaborate necklaces, armbands and jewelled belts, and wears a crown with one or more points. Many of these physical attributes are repeated in the representations of Shiva's consort, Parvati, especially in the marriage scene where the goddess is shown to be almost the same size as her lord. Nor are these physical and iconographical attributes restricted to the god and goddess; even the *dvarapalas*, or guardian figures, flanking the shrine doorways and the wall pilasters either side of Sadashiva, are similarly represented. In a sense, they are the two-armed versions of Shiva himself, wearing the same crowns and jewels.

This limited repertory of conventions by which Shiva is represented in an almost identical manner in all of the panels within the cave does much to link these separate compositions, visually confirming that they do indeed portray different aspects of a single supreme divinity. From this point of view, the triple-headed bust of Sadashiva is yet another version of the god, even though it is much larger in scale, and for this reason concealed from the shoulders downwards. Such a consistency in the figural art of Elephanta is countered by obvious contrasts of posture and mood. These expressive contrasts are skilfully used to illustrate the different aspects of the god: sitting alone in meditation as lord of

Marriage of Shiva and Parvati; the god and goddess are surrounded by subsidiary smaller figures.

Shiva seated together with Parvati in the gambling panel.

yogis, sitting in a relaxed posture next to Parvati, energetically dancing, and violently spearing the demon Andhaka. These transitions from static to dynamic mode are never abrupt, since the panels are spatially separated, one from the other, within the body of the cave. Where they are grouped in pairs or as a trio, they always seem to complement each other; this is especially true for the panels that are set into the rear wall, where Sadashiva is flanked by Ardhanarishvara or Shiva as the Androgyne, and Shiva with Parvati in the Gangadhara panel.

Apart from the larger than human scale, which is such an outstanding feature of the principal figures at Elephanta, there is also a concern with achieving the greatest possible spatial depth. This explains the deep recesses of the panels with figures wrapping around the sides, and the almost three-dimensional modelling of the heads, bodies and limbs. There is, however, considerable variation from the relatively flat and frontal carving of panels, such as Gangadhara, or Shiva bearing Ganga, to compositions in which the figures are almost totally separated from their concave backgrounds, as in Shiva impaling Andhaka. The same is true for the figure of Parvati in the gambling scene, and even subsidiary figures, such as that of the sage Bhagiratha in the Gangadhara panel. Whether such a transition denotes a

Figure of Shiva dancing, showing tilted axes of head and body.

chronological span cannot be determined for certain, but it certainly testifies to the variety of modes in which the Elephanta sculptors were working at the time.

The centripetal scheme, by which subsidiary figures are visually linked with Shiva, is another compositional device that can be found at Elephanta. Axes emerging from the god, in particular from the navel that signifies the centre point of the body, fan outwards in a radial fashion to determine the extensions of the god's limbs, as in the panels of Shiva dancing and impaling Andhaka. These axes also govern the location of the subsidiary attendants and celestials that encircle Shiva and Parvati. The axes even continue to the edges of the recesses, visually compressing the energies of the figures contained within the deeply-cut frame. In the Sadashiva image, there is the effect of an upward ascension, as if the god was emerging from the depths of the mountain. These and other dynamics of the panels imply a subtle geometry that contains and directs the placement of all the figures. Such an implicit scheme parallels that which governs the layout and mathematics of the plan itself.

SCULPTURE PANELS

THE MAIN CAVE AT ELEPHANTA is approached from the terrace on the north. After climbing a few steps and passing between the pair of columns in the middle of the portico on this side, two sculpture panels are seen on the walls on either side. On the left (east) is Shiva as Yogishvara, or Lord of Yogis, seated calmly in meditation, while on the right (west) is Shiva dancing with one of his arms thrown across his chest in a forceful posture known as *lalita*. A more striking contrast of the god's powers could hardly be imagined: as Yogishvara, Shiva's cosmic energy is directed inwards; in the form of the dancer, it is directed outwards.

After these panels, the natural progression is into the body of the cave, towards the immense triple-headed bust of Sadashiva that is carved out of the south wall. Beyond the central east-west axis that runs through the middle of the cave, on which the free-standing *linga* shrine is situated (to the right), is the Sadashiva panel that forms the visual climax of the interior. Here, in this greatest of all representations at Elephanta, the mysteries of Shiva are fully manifested. The panels on either side of Sadashiva depict Shiva as Ardhanarishvara, or the androgyne, to the left (east), and Gangadhara, or Shiva bearing Ganga, to the right (west). Parallel to the contrasts implicit in the pairing of Yogishvara and Shiva dancing, this trio of panels expresses the contradictions that lie at the core of Shiva's complex personality. Here, however, there is the juxtaposition of male and female aspects, either as separate faces, as in Sadashiva, or as individual figures, as those of the god and goddess in the Gangadhara panel. These male-female juxtapositions are only resolved in the combination male-female figure of Ardhanarishvara.

From these three panels, it is but a short distance to the *linga* shrine that serves as the devotional focus of the main cave. Displaced to one side, away from the axis that proceeds from the north entrance to Sadashiva, the shrine is located on the transverse axis that runs through the middle of the cave, linking the east and west entrances. The shrine is provided with doorways on four sides, with light flowing in through them, thereby outlining the curved dome of the *linga* installed within. From these doorways, devotees can enter the shrine and pay their respects to Shiva by taking a *darshana*, or an auspicious view, of the *linga*. Immediately beyond the shrine, lies the western entrance of the cave. The walls on either side of this triple-bayed portico are also carved with a pair of contrasting panels: on the left (south) is Kalyanasundara, or the marriage of Shiva and Parvati, with the celestial couple in the sweetness of their first vows; opposite, on the right (north), is the panel showing Shiva impaling Andhaka with his long trident. This dramatic contrast of peace and violence gives full expression to Shiva's contradictory aspects and moods.

The way out of the main cave into the excavated west court is from here. Directly opposite is a small shrine with a portico provided with sculptures. In order to continue the exploration of the main cave, however, it is necessary to return into the body of the hall, moving around the *linga* shrine and past the great trio of panels on the south wall. Just inside the east entrance, is another pair of sculpture panels. Both of these depict domestic scenes of the god and goddess in their Himalayan home on Mount Kailasa. The composition to the left (north) depicts Ravana lifting Kailasa, thereby disturbing Parvati, while that to the right (south) portrays the celestial couple gambling at dice. The way to the excavated east court is through the triple-bayed portico on this side. To the right (south) is a subsidiary *linga* shrine with worthwhile sculptural compositions.

SHIVA AS LORD OF YOGIS

Shiva as Lord of Yogis, or Yogishvara, enthroned on the cosmic lotus of creation above the world pillar, forms the subject of this badly damaged, but impressive panel. From his earliest appearance in Hindu religious literature, Shiva is associated with those who follow meditative esoteric practices, withdrawing in isolation to rocky caves, as is suggested in this particular panel. As Yogishvara, he is the supreme master of all yogic disciplines, as well as the teacher of all the arts that give expression to an understanding and realisation of ultimate reality.

Though Yogishvara meditates in solitude, here at Elephanta he is not alone; beings crowd upon him from either side within the deep recess of the panel. The fact that they are celestials is

Shiva as Lord of Yogis.

suggested by their flying postures, which can still be discerned in spite of their broken condition. Among these figures are *gandharvas*, or celestial couples, with extended limbs surrounded by billowing clouds, who are seen beside Shiva's head. The upper corners of the panel are occupied by the gods Brahma and Indra who are seated on their vehicles, the goose and the elephant respectively; Vishnu, who is riding on the eagle Garuda, can be discerned to the right of Shiva's chest. Beneath Vishnu is a male figure climbing upward towards the god, but it is much too damaged to be recognised. The same is

Vishnu riding on Garuda, a flying celestial couple and other figures on the right side of the Yogishvara panel.

almost true of the crouching creatures that support the lotus on which Shiva is seated in meditation; however, the serpent hoods which rise over their heads are just visible, thereby identifying them as *nagas*. These creatures flank a pillar-like stalk that visually links the body of the god to the enigmatic world of the primeval deep.

Yogishvara is seated silently in meditation, his legs folded and crossed, with the soles of his feet placed upwards. The hieratic symmetry of his swelling body expresses the inner pressure of *prana*, the breath of life, the control of which is central to all yogic endeavours. The imposing broad shoulders suggest the god's universal strength, as does the silent but magnificent head. The shattered rocky surface that now constitutes the planes of the face does not entirely obscure the eyelids of the god, which

Yogishvara in meditation, enthroned on a lotus seat.

are lowered as he gazes inwards in meditation, nor the rounded modelling of the cheeks, chin and neck. Ringlets of hair flow onto the shoulders; elsewhere the hair is matted into *jatas*, and held in place by an elaborate crown framing the upper portions of the face. A large jewel is placed in the middle of the crown, while a simple necklace graces the neck. The profile of a large oval-shaped halo, conveying the god's divinity, can be made out behind the head.

Of Yogishvara's arms, nothing can now be discerned. However, while comparing this composition with another similar panel of Yogishvara just outside the west court *linga* shrine (see page 75), it is possible to presume that Shiva was depicted here in human form, with two arms only. The left hand of the god would have been folded palm upwards and laid in the lap, while the right hand would have been placed on the right knee. Further confirmation of these details is provided by another seated yogic composition of Shiva in the Dhumar Lena cave at Ellora. This much better preserved sculpture portrays Shiva naked with erect phallus, seated in a yogic posture, holding a club in one hand. It is likely that the Elephanta Yogishvara was also depicted in this manner. Since the Ellora sculpture is generally considered to represent Lakulisha, the Lord with a Club, the twenty-eighth and last incarnation of Shiva according to the mythological collections of the Puranas, Yogishvara at Elephanta is sometimes also identified as Lakulisha.

SHIVA DANCING

The panel of Shiva dancing opposite Yogishvara,
on the right side of the bay inside the north
entrance to the main cave, is better preserved,
especially in its upper portions; even so, parts of
the limbs of the central figure as well as the
attendants at the bottom are lost. Shiva dancing
provides a total contrast to Yogishvara meditating.
Here, the body of the god is portrayed in violent
movement, with the axis of the trunk set at an
angle to that of the head and the legs. Seven of
the eight arms can be made out extending away
from the body, with the first of the right arms
flung diagonally across the chest. Though this
representation of Shiva is popularly known as
Nataraja, Lord of the Dance, this is not strictly
correct. Nataraja actually refers to a particular
dance form of Shiva in which one leg of the god
is raised high off the ground, the other being
planted firmly on the head of a squirming dwarf.
What is probably shown here at Elephanta is a
dance posture with both legs bent at the knees
and both feet on the ground, one of which has
the heel raised up in the act of tapping out the
beat. Confirmation of this particular posture
comes once again from the Dhumar Lena cave at
Ellora where exactly this type of image is found.
In ancient Sanskrit texts on dance, such as the
Nrityashastra, this posture is identified as *lalita*.

Whatever uncertainty surrounds its
iconographic label, there can be no doubt about
what is actually being represented here. Shiva is
shown performing the violent and dangerous
tandava dance that is associated with the
destruction of the world, as witnessed by his wife Parvati in the company
of other gods. This act of cosmic dynamism may be taken as central to the
outer expression of the god's innermost energy, a manifestation of the forces
of the universe in their ceaseless round of creation and destruction. The
body of the god, together with the limbs as they would have originally
appeared, occupies the deeply recessed space of the panel, which is made to

Shiva performing the dance of destruction in the company of Parvati, other gods and celestial figures.

reverberate with visible movement and invisible sound. The latter is implied
by the fragmentary figure of a seated drummer in the lower corner. The
items held by Shiva contribute to the violent twists of his body and limbs.
One of these is a battleaxe with a long shaft around which is a writhing
serpent. The long shaft of the axe that Shiva holds in his rear right hand is

The calm, meditative expression of Shiva defies the violent movement of his body as he performs the tandava dance.

set at an angle that parallels that of the god's head, thereby creating a series of linear inflexions that complement the circular rotation of the outer limbs, now mostly lost. Such compositional devices contribute to the overall dynamic power of the image. Another contributing factor is the cloth held in the rear left hand of the god. This is the end of the scarf that is flicked around the body as part of the dance performance. Whether this cloth is to be interpreted as a veil of illusion unravelled by Shiva in the course of the dance, as some interpreters have suggested, remains a matter of speculation.

Shiva's expression offers a remarkable contrast to this persuasive vision of cosmic movement and energy. The face is calm and detached, the eyelids almost closed as the god gazes inwards rather than outwards. The smooth but broad planes of the face are closely related to the central face of Sadashiva in the south wall of the cave. The crown is sumptuous, with tiers of tassels and jewels containing the coiled *jatas* of the god's hair, except for a few strands that hang down over his left shoulder. Nor is Shiva's jewellery limited to the hair and crown; elaborate earrings hang downwards to drape onto the god's shoulders, while jewelled bands adorn the neck and arms. Such encrustations offer an effective contrast with the fleshy smoothness of the god's face and body. These textural variations are further emphasised by the folds of the cloth placed on the right thigh, all that remains of the elaborate costume that the god wears.

Brahma and a flying couple in the upper left corner of the Shiva dancing panel.

Once again, Shiva is not alone. The deep recess of the panel is filled with figures, a few of which are undamaged. In the top left corner, Brahma can be seen with three of his crowned heads visible, not on a flying goose as is usual, but on a seat carried through the air by a row of diminutive birds. To the rear of the god are two scantily dressed ascetics, while below is the elephant-headed Ganesha with large flapping ears. Ganesha seems to be flying immediately above the standing figure of the war god Karttikeya, recognised by the spear that he holds. Both Ganesha and Karttikeya are considered the sons of Shiva. Karttikeya's link with Shiva is affirmed by the sumptuously jewelled crown and earrings that imitate those worn by the god himself. A damaged seated drummer can be discerned at the bottom of this group. The figures on the right side of the panel include a standing figure of Parvati; her damaged but gracefully posed body is almost lost in the shadows of the deep recess. Above her is Vishnu riding on Garuda, and Indra on his elephant mount Airavata. These groups of celestials are

Karttikeya, Ganesha and a female attendant (above) *on the left side of the dancing figure of Shiva. Two ascetics behind Brahma* (facing page) *on the top left corner of the panel.*

completed by flying figures in clouds arranged in two groups at either side of Shiva's head. As in the Yogishvara composition, the arrangement of these accessory but mostly divine beings clustered around Shiva only serve to draw attention to the much larger single figure of the god himself.

The Eternal Shiva or Sadashiva image dominates the interior of the main cave. Though carved in full relief, the god emerges only partly out of the mountain, with his upper chest and shoulders, two hands and three of his four heads visible. It is this sculpture that forms the climax of the north-south axis, attracting the gaze of viewers from almost every point within the interior of the cave. The huge size of the composition, which is approximately 7 m high, demonstrates the supremacy of this form of Shiva over all other manifestations at Elephanta. However, not only is this triple-headed sculpture the largest of all representations within the cave, it is also

the most puzzling. To begin with, it is necessary to imagine the unseen portions of the image, in particular Sadashiva's fourth face, turned into the rock, and the bulk of his body, including the arms and legs, which is still embedded in the mountain. Some interpreters even postulate an invisible fifth face of Shiva rising above the other four. These unmanifested heads and bodily parts confirm the god's mysterious origins as the lord of the cosmic mountain, at one, physically, with the actual rocky fabric.

The bust of Sadashiva is set in a deep shadowed recess which is devoid of accessory figures or other distractions. The importance of this image is borne out by the presence of *dvarapalas* carved onto the side pilasters that frame the recess. (Elsewhere in the main cave, *dvarapalas* appear only beside

the four doorways of the *linga* shrine that serves as the focus of all rituals of devotion.) The *dvarapalas* flanking Sadashiva are impressively high, though now considerably damaged. They are decked in jewels and wear elaborate crowns containing *jatas*, similar to that worn by the central head of the god. The weapons that they held are now lost, but their *ganas*, or dwarfish attendants, can still be seen. Such creatures form the ever present, impish hosts to Shiva.

Directly aligned with the north–south axis that passes through the interior, Sadashiva's central head faces into

The triple-headed Sadashiva flanked by columns with the impressively tall dvarapalas or guardian figures.

the body of the cave, gazing out through the north entrance to the sea that lies beyond. The overall *linga*-like shape of the head, rising as an almost cylindrical pillar, lends an imposing majesty to the face, which is calm and withdrawn. This magnificent isolation is complemented by the sensuous realisation of the facial features, especially the planes of the deep curving eyebrows and the nose with its broad bridge, the fleshy lips, and the rounded surfaces of the generous brow and cheeks. The eyelids are unarticulated, suggesting that the eyes are closed in meditation, the god's gaze being directed inwards. The monumental simplicity of the face contrasts with the rich sculptural treatment of the triple-pointed crown, with its dazzling assemblage of jewelled settings and bands containing the god's matted *jatas*, which are seen rising above.

The god wears rows of necklaces with pearls and other precious gems; earrings grace the elongated lobes of his ears. One of the hands in front, which can be identified by the worn and barely visible fingers, holds a citron fruit that is rich in seeds; the other hand is damaged.

The side heads of Sadashiva, seen only in profile, are intentionally different from the central head; the one on the left is the face of anger and destruction, while that on the right is more obviously peaceful and feminine. As a trio, these faces represent the range of Shiva's powers, but they only illustrate three of the four faces of Sadashiva. These four faces are identified by some authorities as those of Tatpurusha or Mahadeva (central full face), Aghora or Bhairava (left half-face), Vamadeva or Uma (right half-face) and Sadyojata or Nandin (unseen fourth face). The face of Aghora-Bhairava represents the vengeful and angry aspect of Shiva. These emotions are fully evident in the facial features of the profile, with its slightly hooked nose, twisted moustache, cruel mouth and open eye staring at a rearing cobra held in the single hand. A further expression of the god's angry nature is seen in the treatment of the hair, with its violent curls cascading down over the ear, and the skull and serpent inserted into the headdress, both of which are emblems of death. The face of Vamadeva-Uma is quite different since it represents the female aspect of the god. It is fresh and calm, with an unusually fleshy lower lip; the eye

The aggressive male side head of Sadashiva (facing page). *Female side head of Sadashiva* (above). *The three faces of Shiva* (following pages) *represent the complex and paradoxical nature of the god.*

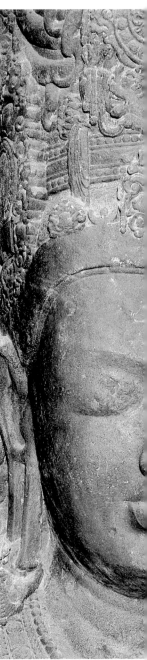

gazes towards a lotus flower held in the hand. The headdress is sumptuous, being composed of festoons of pearls, fresh flowers and leaves. These motifs of feminine beauty frame ringlets and curls of hair.

The contrasts between the three faces that have just been described, underscore the meaning of this profound image. According to the Puranas, Sadashiva is the greatest of gods and the ultimate principle of the universe; he encompasses all that exists, including the unfathomable paradox that lies at the core of cosmic creation and destruction. In this panel, Sadashiva's transcendent powers are expressed in terms of contradictory moods: peace and violence, charm and anger, sensuality and austerity. The incorporation of these apparently irreconcilable moods into a trio of juxtaposed faces is an inspired means of visually realising the inner mystery of the god. This mystery is still experienced by all those who visit Elephanta, as they are irresistibly drawn to the god embedded in his mountain home.

SHIVA AS THE ANDROGYNE

Two complex panels crowded with lesser figures are seen on either side of Sadashiva. Shiva as the androgyne, known as Ardhanarishvara, the Lord Who is Half Woman, appears to the left. An explanation for this unique icon is found in the Puranas. It is written that at the beginning of the world's

creation, Brahma tried to produce living creatures, but they were unable to reproduce themselves, since he had neglected to make women. Brahma implored Shiva to help and he obliged by assuming the form of the Ardhanarishvara, transforming one side of his body into that of a woman. Though the male and female parts were in this way separated, they managed to merge in sexual union, thereby producing all living creatures. In this way, Shiva took over the role of creation from Brahma himself.

The combination of male and female aspects is crucial to the

Head of Ardhanarishvara adorned with jewellery.

Torso of Ardhanarishvara combining the male and female characteristics.

depiction of Ardhanarishvara. Here, Shiva and Parvati are combined into a single composite figure, thereby reconciling the apparently contradictory powers of the god as are manifest in his male and female aspects. The contrasting gender components of the god are clearly expressed, even though the lower limbs of the figure are lost. Ardhanarishvara's right side is clearly male, with a broad shoulder and swelling stomach; the left side is female, as is apparent from the single breast, the curving feminine shoulder, the narrow waist and the exaggerated hip. These sexual distinctions are carried further, into the headdress of the god, which swells above the face and makes the figure somewhat top heavy, partially accentuated by the oval-shaped halo which is still visible. Both the headdress and the halo echo the tilt of the head, which shows the characteristic *jatas* and the crescent moon on the left side, and the more feminine locks of hair on the right; both set within a jewelled crown of sumptuous beauty.

The different emblems that Ardhanarishvara holds proclaim his mixed gender. In the right rear hand he can be seen carrying a serpent, the writhing body of which is still partly visible, while with the front arm he leans comfortably on Nandi, his bull mount. The head of the naturalistically carved animal looks out from the panel. Apart from the head, only its hump is preserved, the remainder of the animal now being lost. Even so, Nandi is a stately presence in the overall composition. Ardhanarishvara holds a mirror in his left hand, which is an emblem associated with Parvati in particular, and female beauty in general. The other left hand hangs gracefully to the side of the feminine hip. None of these contrasting features can be discerned in the face of the god, which remains neutral in gender and calm in mood.

A crowd of lesser beings press in upon Ardhanarishvara, providing the god with a heavenly host of witnesses. At the top of the panel are the usual sets of flying *gandharvas*, their legs splayed outwards in a flying posture, with the cusped outlines of clouds just visible. These celestials to the right are seen bearing garlands above Ardhanarishvara's head. Subsidiary deities are worked into the shadows of the deep recess on both sides of the panel.

The right arm of Ardhanarishvara resting on the head of damaged Nandi (above). Shiva as Ardhanarishvara (facing page), surrounded by subsidiary figures. Flying celestials bearing garlands at the top of the Ardhanarishvara panel (following pages).

To the left is four-armed Brahma, his three heads visible, on a seat carried by a row of geese, as in the panel showing Shiva as the dancer. Next to Brahma is Indra, his clearly carved elephant mount, Airavata, positioned just above the head of Nandi. Beneath these two deities is the figure of Karttikeya, who is recognised by the pile of matted hair, in the style of Shiva himself, with some strands cascading down one shoulder. The spear he bears is mostly damaged. Vishnu and Varuna provide a counterpart to these three deities on the other side of Ardhanarishvara. Four-armed Vishnu is shown riding on Garuda. Though the eagle-like head of Garuda is broken, the wings are seen spreading outwards in deeply cut curving

Karttikeya holding the spear, with seated Brahma above, on the left side of the Ardhanarishvara panel.

planes. Next to Vishnu is Varuna, god of the oceans, who can be identified by the *makara*, or aquatic monster, on which he rides. A number of other smaller figures are seen to the rear: they include an attendant holding a *chakra*, or disc, behind Vishnu, with a diminutive female, possibly intended to represent the goddess Lakshmi, to one side; a dwarf-like creature bearing a water pot also forms part of this crowd. Beneath these, at the bottom of the composition, are two mutilated but seemingly beautiful female figures, one of whom holds a *chauri*, or fly-whisk, across her shoulders. They must be the female attendants of Parvati, placed appropriately next to the feminine left side of Ardhanarishvara. As to their male counterparts accompanying the male right side of Ardhanarishvara, these are now lost.

Vishnu riding on Garuda in the company of other celestials on the right side of the panel.

Shiva bearing Ganga

A no less crowded composition is seen to the right of Sadashiva. In this panel known as Gangadhara, however, the male and female aspects of the god are clearly distinguished in the separate, though unequally sized figures of Shiva and Parvati. More than any of the other Elephanta sculptures described so far, this composition portrays a particular episode drawn from the Puranas: the moment when Shiva receives the goddess Ganga in his hair. It is for this reason that the god in this form is known as Gangadhara, or Shiva bearing Ganga. The story relates how Bhagiratha, a legendary king, was distraught at the knowledge that his ancestors had earned the wrath of the great ascetic Kapila who had reduced them to ashes by the force of his superhuman powers. Consequently, the ancestors were denied access to the heavenly abode unless their remains could be sanctified by the waters of the river Ganga. Intent upon achieving this end, Bhagiratha performed severe and long-lasting austerities, eventually forcing Shiva to agree to his demand that Ganga should descend from the heavens. But since the force of the falling Ganga would have shattered the earth to pieces, Shiva offered to bear her in his *jatas*, thereby taming the goddess and helping her assume the form of a gently flowing river. Thus, Bhagiratha was able to immerse the ashes of his ancestors into the waters of the Ganga, thereby ensuring that they finally reached heaven.

The Gangadhara panel portrays not merely Shiva but Parvati as well. The comparatively well preserved figures of the god and goddess stand in complementary postures, swaying slightly to one side, their torsos inclined towards each other, the heads swaying gently apart. Shiva wears the usual crown, now somewhat worn, as well as a necklace, and a thread that passes over his left shoulder; the belted costume partly covered by a broad sash

The descent of the triple-headed goddess Ganga (above). Shiva and Parvati surrounded by celestials and attendants in the Gangadhara panel (facing page).

Image of Parvati (right) *and kneeling figure of Bhagiratha* (below) *in the Gangadhara panel.*

cannot be completely discerned. The god is four armed, but unfortunately the left arms are broken, though a serpent can be seen writhing outward from the rear armband. With his right rear hand he extends one of the tresses of his matted hair, indicating that he is ready to receive Ganga. Indeed, the three-headed goddess has already arrived above the head of Shiva, her garment billowing outwards on either side as she descends through the air. With his left rear hand, the god gently touches the shoulder of Parvati, quietening her jealousy of Ganga who Parvati views as a rival for Shiva's attention. The kneeling figure of Bhagiratha is seen at the bottom left of the panel, next to the firmly planted cylindrical legs of the god. The inclusion of this legendary king completes the illustration of the story.

In spite of the intrusion of Ganga, the central narrative subject of the composition, it is Parvati herself who is the principal female figure of the panel. The goddess appears as a beautiful woman, with the usual full breasts, narrow waist and broad hips straddled by an ornamental belt. She wears disc-like earrings in her distended ear lobes and is adorned with necklaces.

Her hair is contained in an undecorated crown, with the suggestion of tresses framing her brow. Rather than gazing at her lord, she looks demurely to one side, slightly downward, averting her gaze from the scene that is taking place. Her right arm is bent over a dwarf-like *gana*, as if leaning upon him. This creature, Shiva's impish host, is shown looking upwards to the god rather than towards Parvati; however, a second smaller *gana* to the goddess' left seems to be associated directly with her. As for the items held in Parvati's hands, these are now lost; they probably would have included emblems of female beauty, such as the mirror and a lotus flower.

As in the other panels at Elephanta, there are a host of celestials and attendants surrounding the main figures. Intruding upon the halo at the back of Shiva's head, flying *gandharvas* with extended limbs set in curling clouds appear at both top corners. Here, these couples are expanded into small groups of figures to include ascetics with skeletal bodies and matted hair, their hands brought together in devotion. The usual array of divinities is seen beneath at either side. Carved onto the side wall of the deep recess to the right of Parvati is Vishnu riding on his eagle Garuda; the god holds the mace and disc in his two rear

Parvati with the ganas *or dwarf attendants.*

Brahma with flying celestials above, on the left side of the panel.

hands. In a corresponding position to the left of Shiva is the triple-headed figure of Brahma, next to whom is Indra straddling the elephant. Together with lesser celestials, these deities serve as witnesses to the miraculous incident that lies at the core of this particular myth.

LINGA SHRINE

Away from the trio of panels carved into the rear wall of the cave, stands the square *linga* shrine. This chamber is virtually devoid of architectural features, with simple doorways on four sides surrounded by recessed but plain bands. Steps lead up and through the doorways into the confined space of the chamber, almost entirely filled with the worn plinth into which the *linga* is set. So narrow is the corridor between this plinth and the surrounding unadorned walls that devotees sometimes have to climb up onto the plinth in order to place flowers upon the *linga*. This emblem of Shiva is squat in proportions, being set in a shallow square recess.

The architectural severity of the *linga* chamber is relieved by the pairs of *dvarapalas* that flank its four doorways. These damaged, but superbly modelled male guardians are partly cut out in the round, with their upper limbs free of the walls. Significantly, their crowns almost touch the ceiling of the cave, making them the tallest figures, even larger than those of Shiva, with the exception of the triple-headed bust of Sadashiva. The gigantic scale of these figures proclaims their crucial role as guardians of Shiva's phallic emblem, the principal object of all devotional rites within the cave.

The confined interior of the linga *shrine (above left). The east doorway of the* linga *shrine that is flanked by the impressive guardian figures (above right).*

The *dvarapalas* are portrayed as slender but full-bodied males, swaying slightly inwards towards the doorways, creating pairs of symmetrically disposed figures on each side of the shrine. They wear auspicious threads that pass over their left shoulders and down the bodies, and are decked in necklaces, earrings and armbands. On top of their heads are crowns, with ornate points on three sides, containing the matted tresses, with fan-like headdresses at the back touching the *linga*-like halos. That these guardians are provided with the same crowns and halos as those worn by Shiva in the other panels at Elephanta confirms their connection with the god. Even their refined and detached facial expressions are reminders of Shiva's own expression. As for the clubs or swords with which the *dvarapalas* were armed, nothing survives; the hands holding these weapons are also gone. Except for one of the guardians at the north doorway who is accompanied by a dwarf *gana*, the *dvarapalas* stand in splendid isolation.

The guardian figure or dvarapala (above left) *accompanied by a dwarf attendant or* gana, *beside the north doorway of the* linga *shrine. Arm ornament* (top right) *worn by the guardian. Head of the dwarf attendant* (above right) *and the guardian figure* (facing page).

A few metres beyond the *linga* shrine are two panels carved into the walls on either side of the triple-bayed west entrance. The panel to the left is Kalyanasundara, portraying the marriage of Shiva and Parvati, with the groom and bride standing in the middle of the composition. In this regard, it resembles the Gangadhara panel only a few metres away on the rear south wall. Here, however, Parvati is on Shiva's right rather than his left, and the bodies of the god and goddess incline towards each other, their heads turned slightly inwards so as to be in a gentle communication. Though much of the detail is lost, including Parvati's arms, it is not too difficult to imagine Shiva holding Parvati's hand, an act which is crucial to the performance of the marriage rite. Indeed, this gesture is apparent in the better preserved versions of this scene at Ellora. This Elephanta panel, in spite of its damaged state, still communicates a lyrical sweetness appropriate to the subject.

Parvati was the daughter of Himavant, who is identified with the Himalayas. She was in love with Shiva and wanted to marry him, but she could not succeed since Shiva had taken a vow of eternal chastity. After Kama, the god of love, had tried to divert Shiva from his vows by shooting one of his arrows, Parvati embarked upon a journey of severe and long-lasting penance in order to persuade Shiva. This eventually had the desired result and Shiva agreed to the

Kalyanasundara, or marriage of Shiva and Parvati.

marriage, but first he had to ask Himavant for Parvati's hand. After the formalities were completed, the ceremony took place in the presence of the gods who acted as witnesses of this celestial union, with Brahma serving as the officiating priest.

All of these participants appear in the panel, though as subsidiary figures. Only the upper body of Shiva, who dominates the composition, is complete. He wears the sacred thread passing across the left shoulder and the chest, as well as earrings, a necklace and armbands. There is the usual pointed crown containing the matted *jatas*. The oval-shaped halo behind the head is larger than that in any other composition; its obvious tilt follows the incline of the head.

The graceful but damaged figure of Parvati in the marriage panel.

Only one of Shiva's four hands is preserved, grasping the end of the ceremonial sash that passes beneath the waist. Though the figure of Parvati is much more damaged, her beauty somehow survives the mutilation. The subtle modelling of the breasts, narrow waist and curving hips imbues the goddess with particular grace. A triple-strand necklace adorns the neck, from which a pendant jewel sways over the stomach. The facial expression is gentle and serene, with the eyes downcast in shyness and modesty. Ringlets of hair are seen beneath the crown, with a bunch of piled hair above; one of the disc-like earrings is clearly rendered. The incline of Parvati's head is directed affectionately towards Shiva.

Parvati with Himavant, and Chandra bearing a water pot, on the left side of the panel.

All the witnesses of the celestial marriage are present. Beneath Shiva, in the lower right corner of the panel, is kneeling Brahma performing oblations. Though broken, the multiple heads of the god in his priestly role can still be made out. Behind him is Vishnu, almost lost in the deep shadow on the right side of the recess. He wears a tall crown, but the emblems that he once held are lost. Himavant is seen to the left of Parvati, gently guiding his daughter towards her lord, and leaning forward so as to oversee the rites.

Flying celestials and other figures in the left upper corner of the panel.

A comparatively well preserved figure on the left side of the recess holds a large pitcher of celestial water to be used in the ceremony. The crescent moon behind the head identifies him as Chandra, the moon god. Below Chandra is a much damaged female attendant holding a *chauri* or fly-whisk. *Gandharvas* set in clouds at the two upper corners of the panel are accompanied by ascetics and pot-bellied *ganas*. A single maiden with a long sash in her costume, over Parvati's head, also forms part of this aerial group.

SHIVA IMPALING ANDHAKA

Opposite the marriage panel is the scene of Shiva impaling Andhaka with his trident. This dramatic composition, also known as Andhakasuravadha, portraying the god in the violent act of killing the demon Andhaka, relates to the story in the Puranas that tells of the extraordinary birth of Andhaka

Shiva impaling Andhaka (facing page). *Detail of the upper body of Shiva* (above).

from a drop of sweat that emerged from Shiva's brow, and which was heated up in the third eye in the centre of the god's forehead. Andhaka proved to be an angry child and eventually grew up to be a monster. Unfortunately, he fell in love with Parvati and wanted to abduct her. Shiva flew into a rage and punished him by burning away his flesh and sins with his fiery gaze. However, as Andhaka bled, each drop that fell to the ground caused another monster to be born. Shiva, therefore, gathered the blood in a skull cup. Andhaka finally repented by praising Shiva, who then took Andhaka to his mountain home, accepting him as his son. In return for his loyalty, Shiva gave Andhaka the name of Bhringi, the Wanderer, and made him one of the leaders of his troops. Since Andhaka's blood had been drained away, Bhringi remained an emaciated skeletal figure, which is how he is usually portrayed.

Ascetics and flying celestials above the figure of Shiva impaling Andhaka.

This, then, is the mythological background to the panel. Here, Shiva is depicted in the act of thrusting his trident, with Andhaka pinned to its prongs. Unfortunately, the composition is so badly damaged that the

trident has now vanished and much is left to the imagination. Once again, the better preserved panels at Ellora confirm this and other details of the scene. However, the skull cup held by Shiva in one of his eight hands is still visible, as is the bell and sword in two of the other hands. The two hands at the back hold out the skin of the elephant demon Nila, whose head can be seen to the left of the god. (Nila was a friend of Andhaka who assumed the elephant form to attack Shiva, but was slain by one of Shiva's attendants.) In spite of the absence of the other hands and the weapons that they held, the force of Shiva in this fiendish aspect is

The demonic aspect of Shiva impaling Andhaka.

still effectively communicated. This is mainly due to the dynamic posture, with the body lunging to the right, the left leg lifted up, the trunk turned slightly to one side, and the stumps of the arms fanning out in a radial formation. Though the deeply-modelled torso of the god and what remains of his limbs express Shiva's outrage, it is the face of the god that gives full vent to his anger. Here Shiva is shown with bulging open eyes, a broad nose and a slightly open mouth from which fangs protrude. He wears the usual triple-pointed crown, but this time it is a skull in the middle, rather than a jewel, that serves as an ornament. The matted *jatas* are clearly seen cascading down the left side of the head and falling onto the shoulder. Turned at an angle to the chest, Shiva's head looks out from the panel, but not towards Andhaka whose mutilated naked body can still be made out, seemingly floating above the skull cup held by the god.

As in the other narrative panels, Shiva's act is witnessed by accessory figures. Those in the lower part of the composition are now too badly damaged to be identified, though they probably included female attendants and ascetics, possibly even the kneeling figure of Bhringi to the right. The row of figures that forms a capping frame at the top of the composition is better preserved. Here can be seen ascetics with matted hair on either side of a grotto-like arched motif, in the company of flying *gandharva* couples bearing garlands, with faint indications of clouds.

WEST COURT

From the main cave, a flight of steps between the two central columns of
the portico on the west, descends to the court on this side. To the left is
a large cistern excavated into the rock, which collects water to this day.
(The water is still used by local inhabitants on the island and is also utilised
for washing the caves and their sculptures.) Straight ahead, on the other side
of the court, steps lead up to a triple-bayed portico, beyond which is a small
linga shrine cut into the rear wall. This subsidiary shrine area has two
sculpture panels that are of interest for their comparison with the almost
identical panels in the north entrance of the main cave. On the right
(north) end wall of the portico is the figure of Yogishvara, while on the left
(south) wall is a depiction of Shiva dancing. The Yogishvara composition is
a smaller but better preserved version of that in the main cave. While this

clearly shows a two-armed Shiva seated on the lotus, the club that the god holds in his right hand is lost. There is also nothing of the majestic quality of the more damaged figure in the main cave, giving the impression that

these compositions may probably be a later imitation. The same is true of Shiva dancing, which is only of interest for the female attendants with ornate headdresses. Other sculptures worth noting here are the *dvarapalas* flanking the doorway to the *linga* shrine. They are richly costumed and wear jewelled crowns with elaborately styled hair cascading onto one shoulder. Carved on either side are *ganas* bearing garlands.

In order to view the pair of panels just inside the east portico, thereby completing the tour of the main cave, it is necessary to return to the body of the hall, passing by the *linga* shrine and the great trio of panels on the south wall.

View of west court (top) *with the large rock-cut cistern beyond. The Yogishvara* (right) *and the Shiva dancing panels* (facing page) *on the side walls just outside the west court* linga *shrine.*

SHIVA GAMBLING WITH PARVATI

One of the many quarrels that interrupt the domestic peace of Shiva and Parvati's marriage is Shiva's inability to play dice fairly. In this gambling panel, known as Umamaheshvara, the couple is in the midst of just such a misunderstanding, since Shiva has been winning by cheating and Parvati protests by turning her head away in anger. But this game is no mere domestic entertainment; it is imbued with cosmic significance as the four throws of dice represent the four ages of the world, or *yugas*. By playing dice, Shiva, as lord of creation, subjects the fate of the world to chance; as he always wins, fairly or otherwise, the universe remains under his control. When Parvati protests, Shiva invokes his violent nature, threatening the

heavens, until Parvati finally withdraws her objections and cosmic peace is once again restored.

Unfortunately, the gambling scene is one of the most mutilated at Elephanta, and the head and much of the body of Shiva is now lost. Even so, the deeply-modelled figure of the god, seated comfortably with one leg bent up, leaning towards Parvati on his left, is still evident. Of the head of Shiva, only the *linga*-like profile of the halo behind the headdress can now be seen. The figure of Parvati is also broken, but the full breasts and narrow waist of her body are more or less

Shiva and Parvati gambling.

Parvati flanked by her female attendants in the panel.

preserved, as is the hair, falling in tresses onto her shoulders. She wears
large circular earrings and a double necklace, but the only indication of her
costume that is now evident are some folds on her right leg. Seated in
the same posture as her lord, but noticeably smaller in scale, Parvati leans
slightly away from Shiva, her head turned in a petulant gesture of protest.
As for the items held in the hands of the divine pair, these are now lost.
Parvati is flanked by female attendants, and to the right is the larger male
guardian figure set into the side wall of the deep recess. A similar guardian
is seen in the corresponding side wall on the other side, to the left of Shiva.
Here, too, is another female attendant who forms part of the domestic
retinue of the divine couple.

The details of the lower part of the panel are mostly damaged, though
a group of dwarfish *ganas* can be discerned to the right. The upper portion,
which is comparatively well preserved, is filled with figures. They are
arrayed above a rocky frieze with cubical blocks divided by clefts and even

a grotto-like cavity representing Mount Kailasa. In the upper right corner is a flying *gandharva* couple, their legs extended, set within clouds with curved profiles. They are accompanied by lesser male figures with elaborate hairstyles. Next to them, towards the middle of the panel, is a bearded ascetic holding a begging bowl, with males and females to the side and behind, presumably fellow devotees. Yet other hermits are seen nearby. The left upper corner is occupied by another *gandharva* couple.

RAVANA LIFTING MOUNT KAILASA

The panel opposite repeats the same overall composition, with Shiva and Parvati seated in their mountain home and surrounded by subsidiary figures. The subject of this composition is Ravana lifting Mount Kailasa. While Ravana is best known as the demon king of Lanka who abducted Sita, as related in the epic Ramayana, he is also notorious for his other exploits. One of these brought him to the foothills of Mount Kailasa. Here his path was blocked by a clump of reeds marking the spot where Karttikeya, the son of Parvati, was born. He met with Nandi, Shiva's bull mount, who told him that Shiva and Parvati were making love on the mountain and could not be disturbed. Interpreting this as an insult to his powers, Ravana flew into a rage and, uprooting the entire Kailasa mountain, lifted it up and shook it violently. Parvati was terrified but Shiva merely pressed the mountain down with his toe, thereby crushing Ravana beneath it. However, the demon king was not killed and he

Head of a dwarf attendant (top) in the lower right corner, flying celestials (centre) in the upper right corner, and hermits (left) in the upper right part of the Shiva gambling with Parvati panel. Ravana lifting Mount Kailasa (facing page).

Ravana, the multi-armed demon (above left), *can be seen squatting beneath Mount Kailasa.*
The seated figure of Shiva (above right) *in the Ravana lifting Kailasa panel.*

continued to roar angrily for a thousand years. Only then did he offer prayers and entreaties to Shiva, who finally released him.

This, then, is the subject of the sculpture panel, which, like the others at Elephanta, is sadly damaged. Even so, the deeply-modelled figure of Shiva seated can be clearly seen, his left leg bent up, the other laid flat; evidently the story has not reached the point where the god presses his toe down to suppress Ravana. Shiva has six arms, but only portions of these remain. The head is worn, but the *jatas* can still be seen falling behind the ears. The god's gracefully proportioned torso leans slightly to the left where Parvati is seated. Unfortunately, only the stump of the goddess' body now remains. In the much better preserved versions of this scene at Ellora, Parvati is shown recoiling in terror from Ravana's rage by inclining towards her lord, who reaches out gently to reassure her. It is likely that the god and goddess were portrayed in exactly the same way at Elephanta, but the scene has now to be imagined. Ravana, the protagonist who causes the disorder, is seated beneath the celestial couple. Once again, the Ellora sculptures are helpful in confirming the multiple heads and whirling arms of the demon, which can only be faintly seen at Elephanta. However, some of the blocks of the rocky environment in which Ravana is seated are still complete.

A host of minor figures inhabit the space around Shiva and Parvati, making it one of the most crowded compositions at Elephanta; sadly, the details of most of these figures have deteriorated. Shiva places one of his left hands on the head of an accessory male figure to the right, possibly

Karttikeya, presumably to steady him during Ravana's disturbing rage. An ascetic with an emaciated body is seated nearby, next to Ganesha, with a roughly preserved elephant head, in the extreme right of the panel. The large figure to the rear of Ganesha, with one hand resting on a dwarf *gana*, may be one of the guardians of Shiva's mountain abode. The figures to the left of Parvati, on the opposite side of the panel, are even more worn, but seem to form part of her female retinue. As for the diminutive figures that rise as a great cloud of protective bodies and heads all around Shiva, these can only be identified in general terms as celestials. The usual flying figures in clouds occupy the two uppermost corners.

EAST COURT

Steps descend from the east portico of the main cave into the space of the east court. Considering the prominence of the east-west axis, it is possible that devotees originally approached the main cave from the east court

A view of the east court (below), with the portico leading to the linga *shrine on the left, and the east portico of the main cave on the right. The doorway to the* linga *shrine in the east court with lions on either side of the steps (following pages).*

through the portico on this side. Today, however, the east court is blocked off from the outside and no longer serves as a point of entry.

Larger than its counterpart on the west, the east court is of greater interest since its right (south) side is entirely occupied by an excavated Shiva temple with sculptures of artistic interest. That this subsidiary temple was intended to be co-ordinated with the east portico leading to the main cave is demonstrated by the circular dais cut into the rock floor of the court. The dais is axially aligned with the steps leading up to the east portico as well as with those giving access to the subsidiary Shiva temple on the south. It might be expected that a sculpture of seated Nandi would have been positioned here, facing into the main cave towards the *linga*

shrine within, as is usual in Shiva temples; however, no such animal has been discovered.

The subsidiary Shiva temple in the east court can be approached by steps, which lead to a spacious portico with a large *linga* shrine straight ahead and triple-bayed openings at either end. A further flight of steps gives access to the doorway of the shrine. This is flanked by sculptured lions that were removed from the outer steps a short distance away. The better preserved animal to the right is shown in a seated posture, with its body and one

The sculpted lion beside the doorway to the linga *shrine.*

paw raised up; the expression is fierce with an open snarling mouth. The shrine doorway is composed of recessed jambs and lintels, plain except for the incisions in the outermost band. The shrine interior is occupied by a *linga* on a square pedestal that is similar to, but smaller in scale than that in the main cave.

Leading off the portico is a broad passageway that surrounds the *linga* shrine on three sides. The portico walls on either side of the passageway are enlivened with large *dvarapalas*. The figure to the left (east) is badly damaged, but the *gana* below is sufficiently complete to see the hands on the chest in a typical wrestling pose. The figure to the right (west) is comparatively well preserved. Unlike its counterparts in the main cave, the *dvarapala* has four arms and is shown in a vigorous striding posture with the legs apart. The right rear hand holds an axe, now broken, though a writhing serpent around its shaft is still visible; the left rear hand clutches the end of a garment; the front right hand is lost. The guardian has the same matted *jatas* with flowing curls and elongated ears with earrings, as Shiva himself, but here he wears no crown. A sword can be seen tucked into the belt at the rear. With the front left arm, the figure leans on a large pot-bellied *gana* with a curious pot or cushion on his head. The high relief

The matted locks of the right guardian figure (top). Detail of the guardian's attendant (right).

of the *dvarapala* appears to be an advance on those in the interior of the main cave; indeed, it is likely that it was carved at some later date.

The same is probably true of the sculptural reliefs on the walls of the chamber that lies beyond the triple-bayed portico immediately to the right. A large composition filling the rear wall of the rectangular chamber portrays eight *matrikas*, or mother goddesses. They are shown as standing figures, mostly in slightly undulating postures, bearing children in one arm.

Mother goddesses on the rear wall of the right chamber in the east court.

Since their faces, the emblems that they held in their hands, and the animals or birds that were positioned beneath their feet are broken, it is not possible to identify the goddesses individually. However, the elliptical halos that can sometimes be made out behind their heads confirm that the *matrikas* were considered important divinities in their own right. On the left (south) side wall of the chamber is a depiction of seated Ganesha. In spite of the damaged condition of the panel, the bulk of the god's body and his elephant head can still be discerned. Hardly better preserved is Karttikeya, who is

shown on the right (north) side wall of the chamber, yet he is clearly depicted as a dignified standing figure with two arms only, holding a spear in his right hand. A diminutive figure of seated Brahma is seen beside Karttikeya. Both Ganesha and Karttikeya are surrounded by accessory figures, which include flying *gandharva* couples in the top corners. Though the other lesser figures are too damaged to be easily recognised, their appearance here indicates the status of Ganesha and Karttikeya as independent deities. Traces of paintings on the ceiling of the chamber indicate that the subsidiary Shiva temple may once have been adorned with frescos, possibly like the main cave itself where nothing can now be seen.

Ganesha can be seen on the left wall (top), and Karttikeya on the right wall (left) of the subsidiary Shiva temple in the east court.

SITE MUSEUM

Situated immediately outside the ticket counter to the main cave, this museum was established by Indian National Trust for Art and Cultural Heritage (INTACH) and Archaeological Survey of India (ASI) in 1999 to display the loose sculptures that were discovered on the island. They testify to the other Hindu sanctuaries at Elephanta that have now either decayed or entirely disappeared. The sculptures include standing images of Vishnu and Parvati, a seated female devotee and a beautiful female attendant. The last is of particular artistic interest, especially for the way in which the sari is depicted so as to reveal her voluptuous body. A head of Vishnu with a decorated crown (see page 133) and a small *gana*, or dwarf attendant, are also displayed.

The Elephanta Site Museum (above). *The figure of a female attendant* (left) *in the museum.*

LESSER CAVES

Apart from the main cave at Elephanta, there are six lesser excavations, four on the western hill and two on the eastern hill, numbered from two to seven. Many of these were only partly completed and they have been much damaged by water; compared with the main cave they are of little interest architecturally or artistically and do not attract many visitors.

A short walk of about 250 m from the main cave leads to Cave 2. This incomplete excavation consists of a portico with four columns, off which there are two small cells. Next comes Cave 3, which opens towards the north. Its five-bayed portico, with many fallen columns, gives access to a rectangular hall with a row of shrines cut into the rear (south) wall. A pair of *dvarapalas* flanks the entrance to the most important of these, and a male

figure with six arms is carved on the doorway lintel. A short distance further south is Cave 4, which faces east and is also dilapidated. It consists of little more than a portico with cells at either end, and a *linga* shrine with side chambers at the rear.

A little further on and somewhat lower down the hill is Cave 5, which is only partially cleared, the entrance being blocked by debris.

Across the ravine and on the eastern hill, at a height of about 35 m above the main cave, there are other monuments. Cave 6 has a portico leading to three chambers at the back. A monolithic pedestal occupies the central chamber, but no *linga* or any other image is now seen inside, probably because the cave was used as a church during the period of the Portuguese occupation. About 150 m further on is Cave 7, comprising an unfinished small excavation with three cells. A short distance away, near the summit of the hill, are three wells cut into the rock with small square openings, now much overgrown. A solid brick mound nearby is all that remains of a 10 m-high Buddhist stupa dating back to the 2nd century BC. It is surrounded by seven small stupas and a fort wall built later.

The entrance to Cave 2 at Elephanta.

OTHER RELICS

A number of ancient sculptures of considerable interest have been removed from Elephanta, but deserve to be mentioned here. Other than the life-size elephant already referred to on page 13, there was apparently also a stone horse, which stood somewhere on the eastern side of the hill, near the top of the ravine. This was described by the early visitors, but seems to have disappeared by the end of the 18th century. Among the other relics that were recovered is a four-headed image of Sadashiva, now in the Chhatrapati Shivaji Maharaj Vastu Sangrahalaya (formerly known as the Prince of Wales Museum). Though executed on a much smaller scale than the monolithic example within the main cave, this image shows the same central and side heads crowned with jewels and *jatas*. While the arms and legs are lost, the

torso radiates similar swelling surfaces; most likely it dates from the same period. This also seems to be true of two other sculptural fragments that were found at Elephanta, portraying Vishnu and Mahishasuramardini, now housed in the Chhatrapati Shivaji Museum. Though the head and torso of Vishnu are visible, his four arms are missing. The half-preserved sculpture of the goddess shows her right leg firmly placed on the buffalo demon's body, and one of her left hands holding up the head of the animal so that she can thrust her spear into its neck (see page 94). Significantly, this subject is not found anywhere in the main cave.

Among the portable objects discovered in Elephanta is a copper water jar found in the silt of the large cistern in the west court of the main cave. A short Sanskrit inscription on its neck yields a date equivalent to AD 1068, and gives Shripuri as the name of the locality; perhaps this was the original name of the island itself. Another relic was a small carnelian seal, but this is now lost. As for the stone inscription that was discovered over the entrance

The reconstructed elephant statue in the Veermata Jijabai Bhonsle Udyan (above).
The four-headed image of Sadashiva in the Chhatrapati Shivaji Museum (facing page).

The damaged Mahishasuramardini sculpture from Elephanta in the Chhatrapati Shivaji Museum.

of the main cave and then shipped to Portugal to be deciphered in about 1540, nothing is now known. The same is true of a pair of inscribed copper plates that were reported in the 19th century.

CONTEXT

CONSIDERING THE IMPORTANCE OF ELEPHANTA as the most ancient and splendid manifestation of Hindu art in western India, it is perhaps surprising to discover how little is actually known about the main cave itself. No information is available to identify the patron who ordered the monument or the workmen who were involved in its execution; likewise, there is considerable uncertainty about the religious cult to which the cave-temple was once dedicated. In spite of this lack of fixed data about its historical and religious context, the cave may be architecturally and artistically related to other rock-cut monuments in the Mumbai area, and beyond, in the uplands of Maharashtra. Comparisons with these examples help to situate Elephanta within an overall architectural and artistic development, suggesting a date towards the middle of the 6th century AD.

HISTORICAL BACKGROUND

Other than the inscribed slab that was sent to Portugal and which subsequently disappeared, there are no historical documents of the cave at Elephanta; the only contemporary records of any relevance are those found at other sites. This means that much historical doubt surrounds the monument, assigned variously to the Vakatakas responsible for the Buddhist excavations at Ajanta in the 5th century, the Chalukyas of Badami who ruled from the 6th to the 8th century, and even the Rashtrakutas who commissioned the magnificent Kailasa monolith at Ellora during the 8th century. Walter Spink, an art historian who has extensively studied the rock-cut architecture of Maharashtra, believes that Elephanta is the work of the Kalachuri rulers, in particular Krishnaraja, whose reign coincides with the mid-6th century. The principal evidence for this link between the Kalachuris and Elephanta is the discovery on the island of many hundreds of identical small copper coins. In spite of their decayed condition, the coins have been associated with Krishnaraja, thereby suggesting that he may have been the principal benefactor of the monument. Their uniformly small denomination has led another scholar, S Ghokale, to speculate that they were minted specially to pay the labourers who worked on the main cave.

Spink concludes that during the second half of the 6th century, the Kalachuris controlled the Konkan Coast of western India, where the island of Elephanta is situated, a region which they had seized from the Traikutaka kings some years earlier. According to Spink, the Kalachuris remained powerful in the Konkan until the turn of the 7th century, when they were overwhelmed by the Chalukyas. Though little is known about Krishnaraja, a copper-plate inscription found at Abhona, in the north-western corner of

Maharashtra, describes him as an ardent supporter of the Pashupata sect of Shaivas. Spink believes that the grand scale of the Elephanta monument and the splendour of its sculptures could only have been achieved by a royal figure such as Krishnaraja.

Spink's argument for the Kalachuri sponsorship of Elephanta has been challenged by Karl Khandalavala, another art historian, who believes, together with earlier scholars such as Hirananda Sastri, who wrote an important guidebook to Elephanta in 1934, that the cave must have been patronised by a king of the 6th-century Konkan Maurya dynasty. According to Khandalavala and Sastri, it was the Mauryas, and not the Kalachuris, who succeeded the Traikutakas as the dominant power in the Konkan in the early 6th century. Confirmation of this interpretation comes from the inscription dated 634 on Meguti Temple at Aihole in Karnataka, credited to the Chalukya ruler Pulakeshin II. Here Pulakeshin describes the exploits of his father Kirtivarman, who ruled from 567 to 598, drawing attention to his father's conquest of the Konkan, which at this time was under the control of the Mauryas. The inscription mentions the siege of the Maurya capital, Puri, or the Fortune of the Western Sea. Since the Chalukya invasion of the Konkan does not seem to have occurred until the last years of the 6th century, the main cave at Elephanta must be assigned to the Mauryas. Khandalavala identifies Puri with Elephanta itself, using the name of one of the principal landing spots on the island as evidence: this is the Mora (Maurya) Bunder in the extreme northeast corner of the island, near Mora village. Several European visitors in the 16th century also referred to Elephanta as Puri, thereby suggesting that the island was known by this designation. As for the copper coins of Krishnaraja discovered on the island, Khandalavala proposes that they must have come from a boat carrying pilgrims and traders that was wrecked in Bombay harbour. He points out that Krishnaraja's coins were commonly used as the trading currency on the Konkan, even though the coastal strip was never directly under Kalachuri sovereignty. No coins used by the Mauryas are known.

M A Dhaky is another art historian who concludes that the Mauryas must have been the patrons of Elephanta. He points out that these rulers were only a minor dynasty of local importance, whose domains were absorbed into those of the Kalachuris. Dhaky admits that the history of the Mauryas is so poorly defined that it is not possible to determine a list of rulers. Whether they descended in some way from their more famous ancestors of the 3rd century BC remains a matter of speculation.

This, then, is the debate over the authorship of Elephanta. As neither the Kalachuri nor the Maurya point of view has been established definitively, it must be accepted that Elephanta still remains a historical enigma.

RELIGION

As with the patron and sculptors who worked on the Elephanta main cave, there is much speculation about the religious cult for which the monument was intended, and the particular rites that must have once taken place here. That the cave was consecrated to Shiva is obvious from its sculpture panels, all of which are depictions of the god in different aspects, in the company of his consort Parvati, and his family members, Karttikeya and Ganesha. All of the other carved figures in the panels are clearly shown in accessory roles, including the gods Vishnu, Brahma and Indra, the *matrikas*, and the impish *ganas* and flying *gandharvas*.

While this insistence on Shiva as the sole iconographic subject of the sculptures is fairly common in a Hindu temple dedicated to this deity, Elephanta is one of the few monuments where Shiva in his multi-headed form serves as the pre-eminent visual and dramatic focus. Admittedly, there is no shortage of Shiva temples in which the god is worshipped in the form of a one-faced (*ekamukha*) or four-faced (*charmukha*) *linga*; but here at Elephanta there is a clear distinction between the *linga*, without any faces, placed in its own shrine on the east-west axis of the interior, and the triple-faced image of Sadashiva, housed in its own wall recess, forming a climax to the north-south axis. Such a spatially defined duality, juxtaposing the *linga* and the god's image, is unique to Elephanta, unknown anywhere else in the whole spectrum of Hindu architecture and art.

According to the distinguished scholar Stella Kramrisch, Sadashiva should be thought of as a five-headed divinity, with three visible heads facing into the cave, and two invisible heads, one turning into the mountain and the other rising above. In the Puranas, this cosmic form of Shiva is said to transcend all other aspects of the god. That Shiva was indeed worshipped in this form at Elephanta is evident from the loose sculpture of Sadashiva that was discovered on the island, now in the Chhatrapati Shivaji Museum. Kramrisch goes on to argue that Sadashiva should also be understood as a type of *panchamukha-linga*, that is, a *linga* with four heads facing outwards in the cardinal directions and a fifth head facing upwards. The *linga*-like headdress and crown rising over the central face of Sadashiva within the cave lend credence to this intriguing suggestion. If true, then the cave would have offered devotees the possibility of worshipping two *lingas*, each imbued with a different, though presumably complementary power.

While such iconographic reflections help underscore the complex personality of the god as portrayed at Elephanta, they throw little light on the actual rites that might have taken place within the cave, other than the worship of Shiva in his diverse forms. However, Charles D Collins, the theological historian, speculates that Elephanta was used by the Pashupata sect of Shaivas. He proposes that the sculpture panels formed part of an integrated programme, which emphasised the importance of Yogishvara, who he does not hesitate to identify as a representation of Lakulisha, the founding teacher of the Pashupata sect. When it is remembered that Krishnaraja of the Kalachuri dynasty, who Walter Spink credits with the commissioning of the cave, is known to have been an adherent of this particular sect, then it is indeed possible to imagine that the monument may have been intended for the Pashupatas.

According to Collins, an important and distinctive rite of the Pashupatas is counter-clockwise ambulation, the reverse of the normal clockwise practice of *pradakshina*. In the Pashupata Sutra, an important textual source for this sect, this normally inauspicious movement to the left is favoured as a method of worship, since it leads to the withdrawal of the senses and ultimate liberation, or *moksha*. If, in fact, this counter-clockwise ambulation was followed at Elephanta, devotees might have entered from the north entrance, and proceeded to the right, past the Shiva dancing panel and around the interior of the cave, completing their circuit of the interior in front of the portrait of Lakulisha on the other side of the north entrance. In this way, they would have paid homage to the founder of their sect.

While the Pashupata Sutra and several other related texts offer little commentary on the east-west progression leading to the *linga* shrine at Elephanta's main cave, they do emphasise a three-fold deity who is described as a creator, protector and destroyer: thus Vamadeva, Jyeshtha and Rudra respectively. The attributes of Shiva in this triple form are not discussed in these texts, so they cannot be confirmed at Elephanta. Even so, it is tempting to identify Vamadeva, the beautiful one, with the right or feminine face of Sadashiva, Jyeshtha with the central face, and Rudra, as the cause of fear, with the left or horrific face. In an anti-clockwise progression through the cave, these faces would be seen from right to left, in the same sequence as that described in the texts. The sources then go on to detail the process of worship for initiates to the Pashupata sect, who have to undergo the rites of cleansing and covering their bodies with ashes, followed by several rounds of kneeling, meditating, dancing and circumambulating the *linga* shrine. Unfortunately, there is no way of knowing whether such acts were ever performed at Elephanta.

Whether the Elephanta cave was actually consecrated to Lakulisha, as Collins seems to argue, cannot be confirmed given the overall lack of historical data. The fact remains, however, that the cave interior is visually dominated by the Sadashiva image. In the end, Shiva in this aspect must have been the supreme deity of the monument.

ARCHITECTURAL DEVELOPMENTS

Compared with the doubts that prevent any satisfactory understanding of the historical and religious background of the Elephanta caves, it is something of a relief to discuss its architectural and artistic context. From this point of view, the caves become much easier to appreciate since they clearly belong to a large and well-documented group of rock-cut monuments. This series begins under the patronage of the Buddhists and continues in the service of Hindu sponsors, spanning an overall period of almost a thousand years. While rock-cut architecture is found in many parts of India, only the examples in Maharashtra are referred to here, since they provide the most immediate references for Elephanta. The earliest Buddhist excavations, such as those dating back to the 2nd-1st centuries BC at Karla and Bhaja in the Western Ghats, and Ajanta and Pitalkhora in northern Deccan, take the form either of *chaityas* (Buddhist congregational halls) that are semicircular-ended and roofed with rounded vaults, or of *viharas*, monastic residences with small cells and generally a single shrine opening off a square hall. Both *chaityas* and *viharas* survive with little overall modification and are incorporated into later rock-cut architecture, as at Ajanta and Aurangabad in the 5th-6th centuries and Ellora in the 7th-8th centuries, all of which are located in northern Deccan.

Even though rock-cut Hindu sanctuaries date back to the 4th-5th centuries in other regions, as at Udayagiri in Madhya Pradesh, they seem to be a comparatively late development in Maharashtra. One of the earliest examples in Maharashtra is Jogeshvari on Salsette island on the Konkan Coast, now absorbed into Greater Mumbai. This cave-temple, which probably dates from the first third of the 6th century, is usually associated with the Konkan Mauryas, though this is disputed by Walter Spink. Now in a poor state of preservation and surrounded by slums and garbage, the Jogeshvari monument is partly sunk into the rock and can be approached by two long flights of steps on the east and the west. They descend to small courts open to the sky. Beyond are doorways leading to a large square hall with a row of columns running around a central square *linga* sanctuary with doorways on four sides. This distribution of columns within a spacious hall recalls similar arrangements in the *viharas* of Buddhist excavations, except that here the shrine for the Buddha image cut into the rear wall is moved to the middle of the hall to serve as a *linga* sanctuary. A doorway flanked by windows in the south wall of the hall gives access to a colonnaded portico and another open court, which was left uncompleted.

Rains have eroded much of the interior details of the Jogeshvari cave-temple, but the column forms, with fluted upper shafts and similarly fluted compressed-cushion capitals, can still be made out. As with the *vihara*-like plan, this type of column also derives from Buddhist prototypes. Columns with fluted shafts and capitals may also be seen in the porches of the 5th-century *chaityas* and *viharas* at Ajanta, as well as in the slightly later Buddhist excavations at Kanheri that is only a short distance away from Jogeshvari. As for the doorway decoration at Jogeshvari, this shows side pilasters and lintels with model shrines and *makara toranas* or portals with open-mouthed, crocodile-like monsters at both ends. These portals contain figural friezes, motifs which may also be traced back to earlier Buddhist practices at Ajanta and Kanheri.

The next stage in the evolution of Hindu rock-cut architecture is seen at Elephanta. The lesser monuments on the island, mostly unfinished and subsequently damaged, are also thought to date from the mid-6th century. They employ columns with square or polygonal shafts, with upper circular sections provided with elegant flutings. These flutings continue into the compressed-cushion capitals; the brackets take the form of a simple square plate. The doorways are flanked by pilasters of the same type, while the jambs occasionally have relief bands with setbacks.

The Jogeshvari cave-temple and the minor excavations at Elephanta provide the immediate architectural sources for the main cave at Elephanta, which, as has already been mentioned, is assigned to the middle of the

Fluted columns at Kanheri, left, and Elephanta, right.

6th century. In layout, the cave with entrances on three sides is clearly inspired by Jogeshvari, but here the central hall is expanded into a plan of five by five bays, with additional triple-bayed extensions in the middle of each side to create a stepped outline with 12 corners. Another innovation at Elephanta is the displacement of the *linga* shrine away from the centre point of the hall, thereby permitting a clear axial approach from north to south. Column forms develop those already announced in the lesser caves at Elephanta, with massive square lower shafts and fluted circular upper shafts, providing an elegant transition to the compressed-cushion capitals and the brackets with rolled sides. The doorways of the *linga* shrine display shallow pilasters and relief bands with setbacks, though these are only faintly etched.

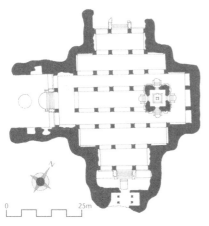

Figure 8 (above): *Plan of Cave 29, Dhumar Lena. The cave* (below) *in late 18th century.*

As for the next stage in the development of Hindu rock-cut architecture, it is necessary to turn to Ellora, a site that came under the patronage of the Kalachuris from about the mid-6th century onwards. These rulers were responsible for Dhumar Lena (Cave 29), one of the earliest of the Ellora series. This cave-temple, which may be dated to the end of the 6th century, is of great interest since it is obviously modelled on that at Elephanta, both in terms of its architecture and sculptures. The Dhumar Lena repeats the same

spacious square hall of five by five bays, with triple-bayed extensions on four sides to create a plan with 12 corners; here too there are excavated access courts on three sides. The *linga* shrine is also displaced away from the centre point of the hall, but here it lies on the principal axis of the cave, opposite the main entrance, rather than to one side (see Figure 8). Dhumar Lena's columns display the identical fluted elements seen at Elephanta, though the proportions are somewhat squatter and less elegant.

For whatever reason, the closely related plan types of Jogeshvari, Elephanta and the Dhumar Lena cave at Ellora were not further developed in later rock-cut architecture. In the cave-temples of the 6th-7th centuries, such as Rameshvara (Cave 21) at Ellora and the trio of excavations at Badami, one of which dates back to 578, Hindu sanctuaries were conceived quite differently as a simple linear sequence of columned verandah, *mandapa* or columned hall, and shrine, the last being cut out of the rear wall. The centralised hall type of temple with a sanctuary in the middle was

abandoned. Even so, spacious halls continued to be an essential component of Hindu temples, as demonstrated in the 8th-century Virupaksha Temple at Pattadakal, which represents the climax of the Chalukya architectural achievement, and its monolithic imitation, the stupendous Kailasa at Ellora. In both these examples, the largest and the most important sculptural compositions are reserved for the outer elevations, which of course was not possible in the excavated inward-looking spaces of Elephanta and the other early cave-temples.

Like the centralised plan type, the fluted columns of Elephanta do not last long in later architecture. While they continue to be employed in Dhumar Lena and Rameshvara at Ellora, as well as in several of the Buddhist excavations at the same site that are assigned to the early 7th century, they soon disappear altogether, to be supplanted by columns with vase-and-foliage capitals. Though of 4th-5th century origin, these luxuriant designs were to become a standard feature of later temple architecture in Maharashtra, as elsewhere in western and central India.

ARTISTIC SOURCES AND INFLUENCES

Not unlike the architecture, the sculptures at Elephanta also form part of a tradition that may be traced back to earlier Buddhist monuments in Maharashtra. This explains the emphasis on pairs of complementary swaying guardian figures on either side of the shrine doorway and Sadashiva, which replicate the Bodhisattvas accompanying Buddha in earlier rock-cut shrines, as at Ajanta and Kanheri. A more specific iconographic reference to Buddhist art can be seen in the Yogishvara panel, which imitates many of the attributes of meditating Buddha, complete with lotus throne and *naga* attendants. There are also stylistic references to Buddhist figural sculpture, as seen in the full rounded torsos and limbs, the faces with fleshy cheeks and lips, the details of costumes and jewellery, the hairstyles with locks of hair falling over one shoulder, and even the halos placed behind the heads. All these features are derived from the artistic traditions prevalent during the Gupta period of central India in the 4th-5th centuries, and which find expression in the painted and sculptural art of Ajanta and Aurangabad. The high relief compositions in the *viharas* at Aurangabad, which are probably contemporary with Elephanta, show a comparable three-dimensional modelling and an emphasis on vigorous posture and facial expressions, best seen in the panel portraying kneeling worshippers in Cave 3. In all these respects, the Elephanta sculptures, in spite of their obvious Shaiva iconography, are undisputably related to this north Deccan Buddhist tradition. As for the Hindu antecedents of the Elephanta compositions, these are more difficult to find.

Hindu subjects are hardly known in the art of Maharashtra prior to Elephanta, mainly because the practice of sponsoring Hindu sanctuaries was little developed in this region before the 6th century. Even the sources of Hindu art elsewhere in India are meagre before this time, being mostly confined to the Gupta period reliefs in the rock-cut sanctuaries at Udayagiri and the sculpture panels of the same era on the free-standing structural temple at Deogarh, both in Madhya Pradesh. While these Gupta period carvings offer valuable stylistic sources for many of the details that are seen in the Elephanta panels, the overall conception of the compositions and the subjects depicted tend to be quite different. This is true despite the fact that there is the same concern with grandiose, larger than human scale, as in the great Varaha relief at Udayagiri.

The Hindu sources, then, of Elephanta's art, are somewhat elusive, and it does not seem possible to pinpoint the precise origins of its technical

Paintings such as Bodhisattva Vajrapani at Cave 1 in Ajanta influenced the sculptures at Elephanta.

assurance, stylistic consistency, iconographic range and enlarged scale. Certainly none of these attributes can be detected in what remains of the reliefs at Jogeshvari. That indeed there was a local Konkan tradition of carving huge Hindu images in relief is demonstrated by the isolated stele at Parel, now one of the suburbs of Mumbai. (A full size plaster copy of the Parel stele is displayed in the Chhatrapati Shivaji Museum.) Almost 3.5 m high, this impressive sculpture portrays a central image of Shiva with subsidiary figures, presumably of the same god, emanating upwards and outwards. The rounded modelling of Shiva in multiple forms, and the high headdresses and elaborate hairstyles are comparable to similar details at Elephanta. Even so, the Parel stele remains an isolated instance, and there is still an overall lack of materials for a fully evolved, local tradition of Hindu art in the region.

While there can be little doubt that the patron of the Elephanta sculptures, whoever he might have been, was responsible for amassing an exceptional concentration of talent under the control of a master architect-artist, there is no evidence of where these artists might have actually come from. The obvious links with the paintings and sculptures at Ajanta have suggested to some scholars that when work at this site ceased towards the end of the 5th century, the artists there might have migrated to the Konkan Coast, possibly to work on Buddhist sites such as Kanheri. Yet, whatever the origins of the artists responsible for the Parel stele and the Elephanta panels, these works of art represent a truly momentous step forward. That the genius of the Elephanta sculptures was fully appreciated at the time is revealed at Ellora, the art of which can only be understood in terms of the previous achievement at Elephanta.

As with its architecture, it is the late 6th-century Dhumar Lena at Ellora that provides the closest reference to Elephanta. Here the walls immediately inside the three entrances of the cave are also converted into deep recesses crowded with full-modelled figures in lively postures. They show many of the same compositions as those at Elephanta, though not necessarily in the same groupings: thus, Yogishvara and Shiva dancing (north entrance), Shiva impaling Andhaka, the divine couple being disturbed by Ravana (west entrance), the marriage of Shiva and Parvati in the presence of the gods, and the couple playing at dice (south entrance). While outsized guardian figures in complementary swaying poses also flank the four doorways to the *linga* shrine, there is no focal triple-headed Sadashiva. Of interest for Elephanta is the isolated smaller icon of Lakulisha carved onto one of the side walls of the Dhumar Lena. This clearly shows Shiva seated on the lotus,

Plaster copy of the Parel stele in the Chhatrapati Shivaji Museum.

the stalk of which is supported by *naga* deities, holding a club in his left hand; the right hand is held up in a gesture that imitates the teaching *mudra* of Buddha. The magnificent proportions of the Dhumar Lena figures and their comparatively well preserved, smoothly modelled bodies and limbs give some idea of how the Elephanta sculptures might once have appeared; even so, they lack the grandeur of the Elephanta reliefs.

The later Ellora excavations continue this tradition of carving large-scale Hindu subjects onto the walls of columned interiors. In the early 7th-century Ravana ki Khai (Cave 14), imposing guardian figures flank the doorway of the shrine, while the walls on two sides are carved with large panels depicting a full range of Hindu gods and goddesses. The scenes of Shiva spearing Andhaka, and the god and his consort playing at dice and being disrupted by Ravana also appear here, but there are many other subjects not found at Elephanta. In comparison with Elephanta, the figures at Ellora are smaller and less dynamic in their postures. Indeed, they bear closer resemblance with the robust, but somewhat static figures carved onto the verandah walls of the late 6th-century cave-temples at Badami. In the mid-8th century Dashavatara (Cave 15) at Ellora, panels cover the walls on three sides of the columned hall. The compositions here replicate most of the Elephanta subjects, but have additional topics, such as Lingodbhava Shiva appearing out of the *linga* to rescue Markandeya, and Tripurantaka Shiva riding in the chariot destroying the demon of the triple cities. The inclusion of a number of Vaishnava images indicates a less sectarian approach to the overall sculptural programme. That there had been a stylistic advance on the earlier models, both at Elephanta and Ellora, is obvious from the exaggerated dynamism of the figures of the Dashavatara excavation, which are imbued with an unmistakable expressiveness. This is best seen in compositions such as Narasimha fighting Hiranyakashipu, Vishnu riding on Garuda, and Shiva dancing. As a final gesture to Elephanta, there are the panels on the plinth and exterior walls of the colossal monolithic Kailasa temple (Cave 16). They include the scene of Shiva and Parvati with Ravana beneath; though damaged, this composition is much admired for the deep modelling and tender embrace of the god and goddess, attributes that have been noticed already at Elephanta.

With the 8th-century sculptures at Ellora, the rock-cut relief references to Elephanta come to an end. After this period, the Hindu artistic tradition of Maharashtra mainly concentrates on pre-carved panels that are inserted into the walls of free-standing structural buildings. While the concern to portray Shiva in multiple aspects continues in temples consecrated to this god, the awe-inspiring scale and the deep modelling of the Elephanta sculptural compositions are lost forever.

If the historical background to the main cave at Elephanta is shrouded in mystery, the same may be said for the fate of the monument over the next thousand years after it was created. During this period, the Konkan Coast came under the sway of successive lines of rulers, both Hindu and Muslim, but nothing is known about the island and the rituals of devotion that took place there. The discovery of a copper jar with an inscription of 1068, has already been mentioned. This dated find suggests that rituals might still have been performed in the cave up to this time. However, this remains an isolated instance in what is otherwise a totally blank era as far as Elephanta is concerned. By the time the cave made an appearance in the historical documents of the Portuguese, it was already abandoned and dilapidated.

In 1534, Elephanta, together with the islands that were to become the city of Bombay, passed into the control of the Portuguese, who were already active on the Konkan Coast. According to Portuguese sources, Elephanta was rented to one João Pires for the annual amount of 105 pardáos (£4),

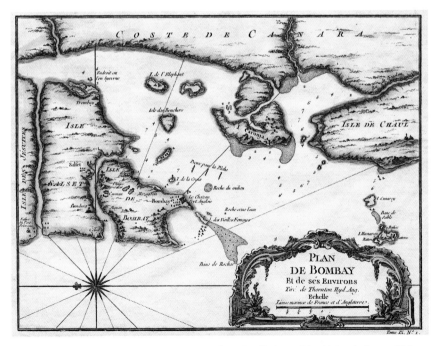

An 18th-century map of Bombay and its environs, featuring Elephanta island (above). An aquatint dating back to 1799, depicting the waterlogged main cave at Elephanta (following pages).

remaining under his control until 1548, when it passed to Manuel Rebello da Silva, who in turn made it over to his daughter, Dona Rosa Maria Manuel d'Almeida. That the Portuguese evinced an active interest in the cave and its sculptures is evident from the accounts of the early visitors. Dom João de Castro, the first to write about Elephanta in 1539, was deeply impressed by the sculptures, even though they were much effected by time and weather. In 1550, Garcia d'Orta found the cave quite damaged by cattle, while in 1579 John Huyghen Van Linschoten reported the cave as deserted and ruined. A later visitor, Diego de Coutto, complained that the sculptures had been disfigured by Portuguese soldiers and that the island's local inhabitants had used the cave as a cattle shed, storing fodder there during the rainy season. In 1712, one of the Portuguese soldiers fired several shots from a big gun into the cave to test the echo, thereby breaking some of the pillars. It has already been noticed that the Portuguese used one of the lesser monuments (Cave 6) on the island as a church.

It is likely that Elephanta formed part of the Maratha dominions for a time during the second half of the 17th century, since Sambhaji is said to have threatened the Portuguese by building a fort there, and even the great Shivaji is said to have visited the island. However, no vestiges of the Maratha occupation can now be seen. Apparently, Elephanta did not form part of the marriage settlement between Charles II and the Infanta Dona Catherina, according to which the islands that were to become the city of Bombay passed into the ownership of the English crown in 1668. In fact, it was not until 1774 that the English took possession of Elephanta by establishing a small garrison there, the task of which was to assist in the defence of the rapidly growing city of Bombay. A battery of overgrown and rusting canons is still seen on top of the eastern hill.

Under the English, the desecration of the cave seems to have continued, and the condition of the sculptures further deteriorated. In 1750, John Henry Grose described the cave as waterlogged, which is how it was portrayed in aquatints by Thomas and William Daniell in 1799. In 1865, the noses of two Sadashiva faces are supposed to have been damaged. Yet not all visitors were vandals; in 1875, the Prince of Wales, later King Edward VII, was entertained in a grand banquet inside the cave. From 1890, the Public Works Department of Bombay began to take steps to arrest further decay of its sculptures, and many of the pillars, which were in a fragile condition, were strengthened and repaired. In 1909, the main cave was declared a protected site under the Ancient Monuments Preservation Act and came under the authority of the Archaeological Survey of India. This organisation is still responsible for the cave, undertaking essential conservation work and sponsoring archaeological excavations elsewhere on the island.

THE DISCOVERY OF ELEPHANTA

During the time when Bombay was owned by the Portuguese and later by the British, several monographs came to be written on Elephanta. Many scholars and travellers who visited the caves wrote about their beauty and mysterious grandeur, while others were preoccupied with the question of their creation. These records serve as valuable documents for the study of Elephanta.

OF THE VERY REMARKABLE AND STUPENDOUS PAGODA by Diego de Coutto

Diego de Coutto, a member of the Royal Asiatic Society, visited the caves around the early 1600s. In spite of having no knowledge of Hindu iconography, he gave a detailed description of these monuments and reported that they were commissioned by a Hindu king named Bánásur, who employed millions of workmen to excavate them.

This remarkable and splendid temple of Elephanta is situated in a small island about half a league in circumference, which marks the Bombay river just when it is about to enter the sea from the northward. It is so called, on account of a great stone elephant in the island, which is seen on entering the river, and is said to have been built by a Hindu king named Bánásur, who became master of everything from the Ganges inwards. It is affirmed (and so it appears) that immense sums of money were expended on this temple, and that millions of workmen were employed on it for many years. The site of this temple stretches from north to south. It is nearly open on all sides, particularly to the north, east, and west; the back lies to the south. The body of the temple is about eighty paces long and sixty broad. It is all hewn out of the solid rock, and the upper roof, which is the top of the rock, is supported by fifty pillars, wrought from the same mountain, which are so arranged as to divide the body of the temple into seven naves. Each of those pillars is twenty-two spans square, and from the middle upwards is eighteen spans round. The stone of the mountain where this temple has been carved is of a grey colour. But the whole body inside, the pillars, the figures, and everything else, was formerly covered with a coat of lime mixed with bitumen and other compositions, that made the temple bright and very beautiful, the features and workmanship showing very distinct, so that neither in silver nor in wax could such figures be engraved with greater nicety, fineness, or perfection.

On entering the temple to the right hand there is a recess sixteen and a half spans broad, and fifteen and a half high. Within are many figures, that in the middle seventeen spans high, with a large and beautiful crown on the head, so nicely made, that it appears to have been painted rather than carved in stone with the chisel. This figure has eight hands and two legs. ... To the left there is another large idol with a cymitar, and over it another very large one, with the body of a man and the head of an elephant, from which I think the island took its name. In this idol they worship the memory of an elephant, whom the Hindus call *Ganesh* of whom they relate many fables. ...

... there is a square room ten paces long and as many broad, hewn in the rock, and so constructed as to admit of a person walking all round. It has a door on each side entered by a flight of five steps. In the middle of the chapel is a square stone seat of twenty-four spans, where there is a figure of an idol so very dishonest that we forbear to name it. It is called by the Hindu *ling* and is worshipped with great superstition, and it is held in such estimation that the Kánarese Hindus used to wear such figures about their neck. A Kánarese king of sound principles and justice abolished this shameful custom. These four gates of this house, the sockets of which still exist, were never opened except once in the year, on the day of its greatest festivity, to show in what veneration they held the idol in question. At each entrance of this house there are two beautiful giants twenty-four spans high.

Ten paces from the chapel going towards the south there is another recess with a beautiful porch of mosaic workmanship, twenty-four feet broad and twenty-six high. ... From this to the west there is a cistern of excellent water, the bottom of which, like the fountains of Alfeo and Arethusa, is said never to have been found. ...

... With this ends the edifice of this pagoda, which is injured in many parts, and whatever the soldiers have spared is in such a state that it is a great pity to see thus destroyed one of the most beautiful things in the world. ...

When the Portuguese took Bassein and its dependencies, they went to this temple and removed a famous stone over the gate which had an inscription of large and well written characters which was sent to the king, after the Governor of India had in vain endeavoured to find out any Hindu or Moor in the east who could decipher them. King Dom John III also used all his endeavours to the same purpose, but without effect, and the stone thus remained there, and there is now no trace of it.

On the side of the hill where the pagoda stands, about two stonethrows to the east, there is another pagoda open in front, and the roof is supported by many pillars beautifully executed, of which only two now exist, and are nineteen spans high and twelve thick. This temple is forty-three paces long and thirteen wide, and at one side there is a small room most beautifully worked. There they worship the goddess Paramisori (Parameshvari). This pagoda, which is now entirely destroyed, was the most stupendous work of its size. ...

Both this large and the other small temples are known from the writings of the Hindus to have been the work of a Kánara king called Bánásur, who ordered their construction, as well as of some famous palaces near them where he resided, of which even in my time there were some marks, and many ruins of cut stones and large unburnt bricks. These palaces or this city, which is said to have been very beautiful, was called Sorbale, and the hill where the Elephant pagoda stands, Simpdeo. A daughter of the king called Uqua, who dedicated herself in this island to perpetual virginity, lived here for many years. The ancients say that during the time of king Bánásur gold rained once for the space of three hours at Elephanta, and it was therefore called Santapori or the Golden Island. *(James M Campbell, p. 84n. 6)*

A NEW ACCOUNT OF EAST-INDIA AND PERSIA by John Fryer

John Fryer, who worked as a surgeon with the East India Company, made a trip to the island of Elephanta between 1672 and 1681. During his visit, he noticed that the elephant sculpture had a young one on its back. Here he observes the square plan of the main cave, describes the figures as giants and blames the Portuguese for their defacement.

Having in a Week's time compleated my Business, returning the same way, we steered by the *South* side of the Bay, purposely to touch at *Elephanto*, so called from a monstrous Elephant cut out of the main Rock, bearing a Young one on its Back; not far from it the Effigies of an Horse stuck up to the Belly in the Earth in the Valley; from thence we clambred up the highest Mountain on the Island, on whose Summit was a miraculous Piece hewed out of solid Stone: It is supported with Forty two *Corinthian* Pillars, being a Square, open on all sides but towards the *East*; where stands a Statue with three Heads, crowned with strange Hieroglyphicks: At the *North* side in an high *Portuco* stands an Altar, guarded by Giants, and immured by a Square Wall; all along, the Walls are loaded with huge Giants, some with eight hands, making their vanquished Knights stoop for mercy. Before this is a *Tank* full of water, and beyond that another Place with Images. This seems to be of later date than that of *Canorein*, though defaced by the *Portugals*, who have this Island also; but no Defence upon it, nor any thing else of Note; it may be Ten Miles round, inhabited by the *Povo*, or Poor: From hence we sailed to the *Putachoes*, a Garden of Melons (*Putacho* being a Melon) were there not wild Rats that hinder their Growth, and so to *Bombaim*. *(pp. 75-76)*

A VOYAGE TO SURATT IN THE YEAR 1689 by J A Ovington

J A Ovington was a chaplain with the East India Company, Surat. Here he discusses the pagoda or the main cave at the top of the hill, describing the sculptures within, and believes that the statues at Elephanta represented gigantic forms of the first race of mortals.

At three leagues distance from Bombay is a small island called Elephanta, from the statue of an elephant cut in stone, in equal proportions to one of those creatures in his full growth. This figure is placed in the middle of a field, conspicuous to any passenger that enters upon that part of the island. Here likewise are the just dimensions of an horse carved in stone, so lively, with such a colour and carriage, and the shape finisht with that exactness, that many have rather fancyed it, at a distance, a living animal, than only a bare representation. These figures have been erected not barely for displaying the statuary's skill, or gratifying the curiosity of the sight, but by their admirable workmanship were more likely designed to win upon the admiration, and thereby gain a kind of religious respect from such heathens as came near them.

But that which adds the most remarkable character to this island, is the famed Pagode at the top of it; so much spoke of by the Portuguese, and at present admired by the present Queen Dowager, that she cannot think any one has seen this part of India, who comes not freighted home with some account of it. A Pagode is the heathens temple, or a place dedicated to the worship of their false gods, and borrows its name from the Persian word Pout, which signifies idol; thence Pout Gheda, a temple of false gods, and from thence, Pagode.

At the ascent of an high hill upon this island Elephanta, is therefore a very large Indian Pagode, cut out of the very heart of a hard rock, whose dimensions are about an hundred and twenty foot square, and in height about eighteen; besides several out-rooms appertaining and adjoining to it. At sixteen foot distance from one another are sixteen pillars of stone, cut out with much art and ingenuity, whose diameters are three foot and an half, designed as it were for the support of this weighty building, whose roof is a lofty broad rock. Out of the sides of this Pagode, thus beautified with these lovely columns and curious arches, are figures of forty or fifty men, each of them twelve or fifteen foot high, in just and exact symetry, according to the dimensions of their various statures. Of these gigantic figures, some had six arms, and others three heads, and others of such vast monstrosity, that their very fingers were larger than an ordinary man's leg. Upon some of their heads were ornamental crowns, neat and artificially wrought, whilst others near them held scepters in their hands, and above the heads of others are multitudes of little people represented in a posture of devotion; some I observed leaning upon women, and others upon the head of a cow, an animal most venerable in India. Here are some taking an amiable charming lady by the chin, and there the horrid prospect of others hewing in pieces little children; and generally above the heads of all, are abundance of diminutive folk hovering in the air, represented with chearful aspects, and in lively figures. This variety of pleasant and monstrous images, I lookt upon as no other than the several objects of the Gentiles worship, as each adorer's fancy led him to his several god, either of terror or delight.

There is nothing of beauty in the frontispiece of this Pagode, or of ornament at the entrance into it. The figures of these gigantic men, to which the heathen have paid a profound veneration, and reverenced as heroes or demi-gods formerly, (for this island is at present in the possession of the Portuguese) are the representation of the first race of mortals, which, according to the account of their chronicles, were all gyants, but ... through the degeneracy of manners, which caused an universal decay of nature, they shrunk into these small proportions in which they appear now. ... So that the present smallness of our stature, according to them, derives its declension and decay from the excess of vice, and the small remains of vertue that are left. And because the forming of a temple out of such hard matter, required incredible endless pains, therefore they would insinuate that these giants here expressed, were only capable of such performances, which seem now to exceed that ordinary strength we have now to go through with such a work. *(pp. 70-71)*

ORIENTAL MEMOIRS by James Forbes

James Forbes, a writer with the East India Company, arrived in Bombay in 1766. Here he talks about his visit to the caves with an English artist who is rendered speechless by their beauty.

The island of Elephanta, about two leagues from Bombay, does not exceed three miles in circumference; consisting of two rocky mountains, covered with trees and brush-wood, and a small valley of rice-fields ... whose cottages and cattle enliven the scene. Near the landing place is the figure of an elephant the size of life, shaped out of a rock, which probably gave its name to the island; that by which the natives distinguish it being very different.

Ascending the mountain by a narrow path, winding among rocks, trees, and underwood, we arrive at the excavation, which has long excited the attention of the curious, and afforded ample scope for the discussion of antiquarians. ...

I once accompanied an eminent English artist on his first visit to the Elephanta; I had been lavish in its praise; too much so, as I had reason to conclude, on our arrival at the great temple. After the glare of a tropical sun, during the walk from the landing-place, it was sometime before the eye had accommodated itself to the gloom of these subterraneous chambers sufficiently to discriminate objects in that sombre light. We remained for several minutes without speaking, or looking particularly at each other: at length, when more familiarized to the cavern, my companion still remained silent, I expressed some fear of having been too warm in my description, and that, like most other objects, the reality fell short of the anticipated pleasures: he soon relieved my anxiety by declaring, that, however highly he had raised his imagination, on entering this stupendous scene he was so absorbed in astonishment and delight as to forget where he was. He had seen the most striking objects of art in Italy and Greece, but never anything which filled his mind with such extraordinary sensations. So enraptured was he

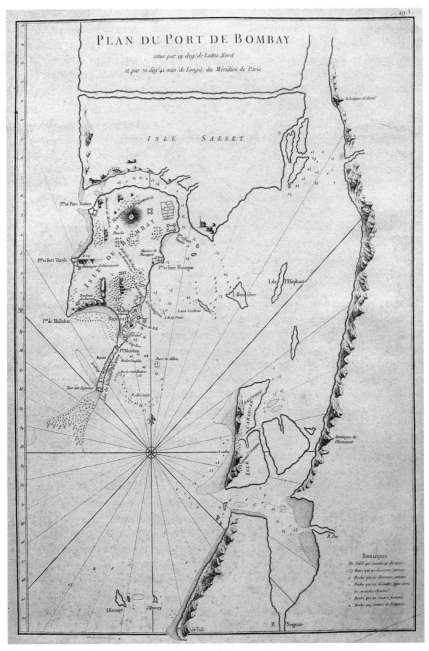

An 18th century plan of the port of Bombay featuring Elephanta island.

with the spot, that after staying until a late hour he reluctantly accompanied me to the hospitable mansion of an English officer at Butcher's island; whither we repaired every evening, and returned on the following morning to revisit Elephanta, as the nocturnal damps render it dangerous to sleep in the caverns, and the cottages of the natives cannot accommodate Europeans.
(Vol. I, pp. 429, 431, 433)

VOYAGES AND TRAVELS TO INDIA by Viscount George Valentia

George Valentia left Britain in 1802, setting out on an exploration of India and the neighbouring countries that lasted four years. Here he praises the skilful execution of the stone sculptures at Elephanta and wonders what they must have looked like in their unspoiled state.

I was afterwards tempted by the verdant appearance of the Island of Elephanta, which rears its woody head nearly in the centre of the bay, as much as by the report of its celebrated cave, to pay it a visit. The accurate Niebuhr has given so good an account of it, that a description is unnecessary. I have only to observe, that I do not think either his drawing, or the etching in the Asiatic Researches, have given the character of the triune deity. Brahmah's countenance admirably expresses the undisturbed composure of the creator of the world; Vishnou's, on the left, has every feature of benevolence, while the lotus which he holds in his hand seems to be expanding under the genial ray of his eye. Seva's, on the contrary, has a ghastly and dire scowl, that well accords with the objects that he holds before him, two of the most venemous of serpents, the covra copel. I was much surprised at the ingenuity of the conception, and the merit of the execution, of these figures. How superior must they have appeared when in a state of perfection!

It was pleasing to me to find, that the great cave of Elephanta, which opens to the north, and has a flat roof, had no inscription in the unknown character, nor any figure of Boodh. Of the numerous deities of the Hindoo mythology, many have been honoured with a place; but the most curious figure, and which has been noted by every traveller, is that of a female amazon, which, from having four arms, most probably represents some super-human personage. Did the romance of the Amazons reach Greece from India, or were there ever such personages in the Eastern world are interesting questions, but at present incapable of solution. There is no appearance of any great violence having been used to injure the figures. Had cannon been employed by the Portuguese for that purpose, the marks of the balls would have been visible, and the destruction would have been among the figures. As it is, the pillars are more rapidly decaying than any other part. The water is permitted during the rains to lodge in the cave, and the stone, being a soft one, moulders perceptibly away in the vicinity of the open air. The scene, from the little level space in front, is extremely beautiful, and a cool breeze tempers the heat in the most sultry day of summer. The beauty of the place has however been considerably diminished by a wall, which has been erected across the front, to prevent cattle from getting in, and, as I hear, to prevent curious visitors also from treacherously carrying off the legs, heads, and arms of these helpless deities. *(Vol. II, pp. 199-200)*

TRAVELS IN VARIOUS COUNTRIES OF THE EAST by Sir William Ouseley

While accompanying Sir Gore Ouseley on a diplomatic mission to India from London, Sir William Ouseley visited Elephanta in 1811. Here he describes how he climbed the head of Sadashiva to ascertain if there was a fourth face.

But every thing seen in the great excavation at *Keneri*, though all traces of its date and origin have disappeared in the obscurity of ages, seemed to me less ancient than the sculptured deities, astonishing by their magnitude, their multiplicity and extraordinary forms, those who visit the stupendous cavern-temple of *Elephanta*. To this, early on the twenty-seventh, Sir Gore Ouseley with a numerous party of gentlemen, proceeded in Mr. Money's commodious and handsome yacht. The small island which contains this cavern, is seven or eight miles distant from Bombay, and owes its European name above mentioned, to a conspicuous figure near the landing-place, hewn out of stone once solid, but now much injured, representing an elephant of considerable size. The island, as some one observed, is properly denominated *Gharipuri*.

About half a mile from the elephant, we arrived at that hill of hard rock, which contains the celebrated excavation. Of this, so many accounts have been already published, that little remains for me to add from a very hasty inspection. But a drawing made at my request, by Major D'Arcy...will supply the place of verbal description. It shows the immense columns, the bust with three faces, and other sculptures, all parts of the solid stone; while portraits of some gentlemen, actually present, which Major D'Arcy has introduced, sufficiently indicate the relative proportions. That there never had been an opening behind the triple-visaged head, nor a fourth face, as some have imagined, I ascertained by climbing to the summit, and convincing myself that this entire mass belonged to the rock from which it projects in bold relief, but never was wholly separated.

On my left, when standing opposite to this bust, I soon perceived in a compartment which exhibits various groups, that form of gigantick size, by many supposed to represent an Amazon, as it wants the right breast; a defect, perhaps not originally intended by the artist, but caused by that violence which has here defaced and mutilated several other sculptures.

Believing it, however, so designed at first, a learned antiquary discovers in this four-handed giant, an androgynous Bacchus; while, according to an ingenious mythologist, it is a figure combining the God MAHADEVA, and the Goddess PARVATI; although a friend, well acquainted with the usual attributes and aspects of *Hindú* deities, immediately pronounced it to be DURGA, who appears, in some instances, the same as PARVATI herself. The plate (V)

affords a glimpse of this figure, seen in the obscure excavation: one hand resting on the head of a bull; but it did not, by any means, recall to my imagination, those forms with which the Greeks or Etruscans invested their Amazons on monuments still preserved: nor does it agree with the description of those warlike females left by Persian writers, and to be examined in a future work on the history of Alexander. *(Vol. I, pp. 81-84)*

ACCOUNT OF THE CAVE-TEMPLE OF ELEPHANTA by William Erskine

William Erskine visited Elephanta in 1813 and spent ten days in the caves. Here he observes the sculptural style and the remnants of paintings on the roof.

Travellers have entertained very different ideas of the degree of genius and art displayed in this temple and the figures around it: some are disposed to ... speak in rapturous terms of the execution and design of several of the compartments. To me, it appears, that while the whole conception and the plan of the temple is extremely grand and magnificent, and while the outline and disposition of the separate figures indicate great talent and ingenuity, the execution and finishing of the figures in general (though some of them prove the sculptor to have had great merit) fall below the original idea, and are ... in no instance being possessed of striking excellence. The figures have something of rudeness and want of finish, the proportions are sometimes lost, the attitudes forced, and every thing indicates the infancy of the art—

though a vigorous infancy. The grouping appears to be still more defective than the execution of the separate figures:—a number of little and almost dwarfish figures are huddled around one or two larger ones. Indeed it deserves consideration, whether the nature of the Hindû mythology, which represents every thing by hieroglyphic, be not extremely unfavourable to the fine-arts. ...

It is worthy of notice, that the excavation appears once to have been painted in water-colours: some of these colours still adhere to the roof, though none of the figures that have been painted on it are so entire as to be recognisable. Some remains of water-colours are also visible in other parts of the caves. It is probable that all the figures were once painted in many and glaring colours, as is still practised in regard to Hindu idols. The third eye in the forehead of Shiva and of his servants could not have been distinguished at any considerable distance unless painted. ...

Over the grand entrance, between the eastern pillar and pilaster, there is a drawing in water-colours of several concentric circles with some figures, which may have represented the signs of the zodiac; but the colours are too much worn out to admit of their being correctly distinguished. *(pp. 245, 247)*

NARRATIVE OF A JOURNEY THROUGH THE UPPER PROVINCES OF INDIA
by Reginald Heber

Reginald Heber was the first bishop of Calcutta. When he visited Elephanta in 1825, he was overwhelmed by the unexpected beauty of the caves and the island. Here he mentions that the elephant has deteriorated and the young one on its back is no longer visible.

On the 8th [May] we went to see Elephanta, of which my wife has given an account in her journal, and of which a more regular description is needless. ...I will only observe that the Island of Elephanta, or Shaporee, is larger and more beautiful than I expected, containing, I should suppose, upwards of a thousand acres, a good deal of which is in tillage, with a hamlet of tolerable size, but the major part is very beautiful wood and rock, being a double-pointed hill, rising from the sea to some height. The stone elephant, from which the usual Portuguese name of the Island is derived, stands in a field about a quarter of a mile to the right of the usual landing-place. It is about three times as big as life, rudely sculptured, and very much dilapidated by the weather. The animal on its back, which Mr. Erskine supposes to be a tyger, has no longer any distinguishable shape. From the landing-place, a steep and narrow path, but practicable for palanquins, leads up the hill, winding prettily through woods and on the brinks of precipices, so as very much to remind me of Hawkstone....though my expectations were highly raised, the reality much exceeded them, and that both the dimensions, the proportions, and the sculpture, seemed to me to be of a more noble character, and a more elegant execution than I had been led to suppose. Even the statutes are executed with great spirit, and are some of them of no common beauty, considering their dilapidated condition and the coarseness of their material. *(Vol. III, pp. 79-80)*

Detail of an engraving depicting the elephant with an indistinguishable shape on its back, that once stood on the island of Elephanta.

REPORT ON THE ELURA CAVE TEMPLES AND THE BRAHMANICAL AND JAINA TEMPLES IN WESTERN INDIA by James Burgess

James Burgess, an archaeological surveyor and reporter to the British government for western and southern India, visited the caves around the mid-19th century. Here he compares the capitals and pillars at Elephanta with their Greek counterparts, as well as with other Hindu temples, particularly Ellora.

The great cave at Elephanta, in the Bombay harbour, has been so long known to Europeans, and has been consequently so often described and so fully illustrated by Daniell and others, that it is hardly necessary to say anything about it in the present work.

The cushion-shaped capitals which crown all its pillars...seems to have reached its greatest development and beauty of form in this cave, but is found in greater or less perfection in so many caves dating from before and after this one, that it has come to be considered the typical capital of Indian architecture. It may be compared with the Doric style of classical art...as exemplified in the Râmêśvara [at Ellora] and elsewhere, may be considered as a richer Ionic order. The two are the principal forms or "orders" of Indian art, and though they may be compared with the classic orders, they are thoroughly original in their form and indigenous in their inception.

The Elephanta cushion capital is also of interest, as being the same form that constitutes the *amalâ śila* or *amalâka* crown to Hindu temples of the same age; and though we are still unable to guess from what it may have been derived, we can hardly escape the conviction that their origin was the same.

In some respects the Dumar Lena at Elura may be said to be a finer cave than this, as it is a larger one, but it wants that perfection of finish both in architectural and sculptural details which make this temple so remarkable and so justly admired. The third of the group—the Jôgêśvari one—both as regards its architecture and sculpture, is greatly inferior, and probably may be considered as the last of the class....

But, besides the great cave, there are several others on the island, which seems to have been a very early sacred place; for, on the north-east of it, on its highest point, is a large ruined brick Bauddha stûpa, which I had opened in May 1882, but found no relic chamber in it. *(pp. 55-56)*

LECTURE ON THE RELIGIOUS EXCAVATIONS OF WESTERN INDIA by John Wilson

John Wilson, a Scottish missionary and scholar, visited Elephanta in 1850. In the following excerpt, he gives a detailed description of the magnificent sculpture of Sadashiva.

Even our own learned Faber, so late as 1803, founding on the descriptions of Elephanta given by Mr. Maurice and others, could indite the following nonsense:—'The five-headed Brahmá [two heads are *imagined* to be behind the three of the *trimúrtí* seen by visitors] is an hieroglyphical representation of Noah, his three sons, and his allegorical consort the ark. At the termination of the deluge, the patriarch lost his fifth head, the ark [as Brahmá did in the Hindu legendry], which ... was said to have been cast off by him that moves upon the waters; but from the blood which flowed from it the whole race of animals was reproduced; or ... the animals which were destined to stock the new world issued from the womb of the ark. The cavern of Elephanta, then, being ... a helio-arkite grotto, we shall find no difficulty in discovering the reason why the compound bust of Noah and his three sons was placed within it; why precisely eight figures guarded the doors; and why the disgraceful symbols of Bacchus, Attis, Osiris, or Mahádeva occupied so conspicuous a place in the sacellum.' ...

A characteristic example of the Brahmanical caves is to be found at *Elephantá*, the well-known, beautiful, and easily accessible island in the Bombay Harbour, with the form, size, and appearance of which very many are doubtless familiar. We confine our remarks upon these caves at present to their principal mythological sculptures and their import.

Fronting the entrance of the large temple, but at its extremity, is the great *trimúrtí*, or image with three heads combined together, about nineteen feet in height, though it extends only from the shoulders upwards. This is *Shiva* possessed of the three functions—of creation, preservation, and destruction just alluded to, and personified with the active attributes ascribed respectively to Brahmá, Vishnu, and Shiva. The front face is that of Shiva as *Brahmá*, the god of prayer or the word, in whom the creative energy is thought to centre. The face to the right of the spectator is that of Shiva as *Vishnu*, the god of preservation, recognized by his purer appearance and his symbol, the lotus. The face to the left of the spectator is that of *Shiva*, as the destroyer, recognized by his fiercer aspect, the feline moustache, the slabbering lip, the terrific serpents in his hand and forming his hair, his prominent brow, and the skull near his temples. This composite bust, which is unique in point of size and execution, is remarkable for its head-dresses representing simple royal *mukatas* or diadems with pearl pendents and precious stones set in gold or silver, and necklaces and earrings and other ornaments mixed with curled locks, which throw light on the capital and thoracic adornments of the kingly natives before the introduction of the turban. It was almost perfect till a few years ago, when some thoughtless or mischievous visitors broke off a portion of the noses of two of the figures. Though it represents a triad of comparatively modern invention, it is in unison with such a triad of deities as the Hindus, like other ancient peoples, have been familiar with from the earliest times. We say distinctively a triad, for the detachment of the figures from the rock above shows plainly that no more than three faces were intended. *(pp. 11-12, 27-29)*

THANA: PLACES OF INTEREST by James M Campbell

James Campbell, a civil servant, visited the caves in the late 19th century. Here he describes the celebration of the festival of Shivaratri in these caves and presumes that they must have once been painted like those at Ajanta.

Though it has long lost almost all its people and almost all its holiness, Elephanta, perhaps from about the third to about the tenth century, was the site of a city and a place of religious resort. The Great Cave about half way up the north face of the western block of hills is the chief object of interest. Besides the Great Cave there are, in the rice fields to the east of the northern or Shet bandar landing place, brick and stone foundations, broken pillars, and two fine fallen statues of Shiv. About 200 yards to the south-east of the Great Cave and almost on the same level, are two large much ruined caves. On the crest of the hill, above the Great Cave, is a broken stone lion or griffin, probably originally one of the warders of the main entrance door to the Great Cave. Near the shore, to the south of the range between the two blocks of hills, are the small village of Ghárápuri, the dry bed of a pond, an uninscribed stone with the ass-curse, the old landing-place, the ruins of a Portuguese watch-tower, the site of the huge rock-cut elephant that gave the island its European name, and several large *lings* square below and conical above. ...

On the shore about 100 yards east of the pier, under some trees, are the remains of a statue of Shiv and of another figure apparently an attendantz ... About 200 yards further to the south-east ... is a well-carved five-headed image of Shiv. ...

At first view the inside of the cave seems full of a confusing number of lines of plain massive pillars running at right angles, with side aisles and porches leading to open courtyards. On the right centre of the hall the lines of pillars are broken by a raised and walled shrine or chapel, and in the south wall are dark recesses filled with groups of colossal figures. ...

The face to the left or east is Shiv as Rudra. ... The nose is Roman and the upper lip is covered with a moustache, the mouth is slightly open with an amused, perhaps *bháng*-intoxicated look, showing the tip of the tongue and perhaps a tusk or long tooth. ...

On the walls of the recess are traces of the cement painted with water colours with which ... the whole cave was covered. The bust shows no sign of colour. If they were coloured, Brahma was white, Rudra black, and Vishnu red. ...

There is no inscription in the caves. It is hoped that the date and name of the builders may be learned from a stone which was taken to Europe about 1540 by the Portuguese Viceroy Dom João de Castro, and which may still be found in Portugal, and deciphered. ...

Besides the stories that they are the work of the Pándavs, or of. ... Alexander the Great, the Musalmán Pándav or King Arthur ... a local tradition [states] that the caves were cut by a Kánara king named Bánásur, whose daughter

Usha dedicated herself to perpetual virginity and lived on the island for many years. Besides the caves, Bánásur is said to have built many mansions on the island, and a beautiful palace at a city called Sorbale....

When new the walls and ceiling of the caves, and probably as at Ajanta and Kanheri the pillars and figures, were covered with a coating of painted cement. The caves probably continued well cared for till the overthrow of the Devgiri Yádavs by Alá-ud-din Khilji (1295-1316) at the close of the thirteenth century. At the beginning of the sixteenth century, perhaps during the greater part of the fifteenth century, Elephanta, with the rest of the Thána coast, was nominally under the Musalmán kings of Ahmedabad. They do not seem to have interfered with the caves, which, when they passed to the Portuguese in 1534, were the best of all the cave temples, as big as a monastery, with courts and cisterns, and, along the walls, many sculptures of elephants, tigers, human beings, and other cleverly figured images well worth seeing....

From the time of the Portuguese conquest till within the last few years, Elephanta seems to have almost ceased to be a Hindu place of worship. In 1854 a Lohána of Bombay, at a cost of £1200 (Rs. 12,000), built the flight of steps that leads from the north shore to the Great Cave.... On Shiv's great day in February (Mágh vadya 13th) a fair is held and the ling in the central shrine worshipped. The last fair (16th February 1882) was attended by about 900 pilgrims, half of whom entered the caves and approached the images.

The rest, unable or unwilling to pay the entrance charge of 6d. (4 as.), contented themselves with bowing to the gods from the mouth of the cave. The pilgrims were mostly Maráthás, Sonárs, Kásárs, Kámáthis, and Bhandáris from Bombay, Sálsette, and Panvel. The officiating priest was a Bombay Gosávi who was helped by four Ágris, dwellers on the island. Besides the worshippers from the neighbouring Marátha country there was a body of Gujarát Vánis who brought a Gujarát Bráhman as their priest. The images worshipped were the three-faced bust, the lings, and almost all the statues of Ganesh or Ganpati. The favourite part of the cave is the east wing, where a pool of water on the floor of the eastern recess or chapel is believed to be sent from the Ganges in honour of Shiv's great day. Several of the figures, especially the two statues of Ganesh, in the curious Mátrika chamber in the west wall of the same cave are also worshipped. The worship consists of pouring water over the images, burning incense before them, offering bel, Ægle marmelos, leaves to the lings, and smearing Ganpati and some other figures with redlead. The total number of visitors to the caves in 1880-81 was 5400....

Above these caves, at the end of a thickly wooded spur that runs north from the main range, a little to the west of the Great Cave, is a rock-carved tiger which is worshipped as Vágheshvari or the Tiger Goddess. It stands about two feet high and is one foot nine inches across the hams. Round the neck is a collar. The head is nearly perfect and the figure is preserved though the rock is split in several places. It is much like the tiger or lion guards on the steps to the east wing of the Great Cave, and, in Dr. Burgess' opinion, is probably one of the two warders of the north or main entrance of the Great Cave whose pedestals may still be traced. Dr. Wilson notices that this tiger is mentioned in the twenty-ninth chapter of the first section of the *Sahyádri Khand* of the *Skanda Purána*, it probably is the origin of Simpdeo, or Singhdev, De Couto's name for the hill in which the Great Cave is cut. ...

About 100 yards east of the pond, near the foot of the east spur, is the village of Ghárápuri a hamlet of twenty thatched wattle and daub houses. ... Near the headman's house was found a fragment of a small well carved and graceful figure of a woman suckling a baby. The child and the mother's arms are unharmed, but her head and all below the waist are gone. She wears four plain bracelets, and the ends of a shawl or upper robe hanging in front of her shoulders are cut with much skill. Close to the village, on a mound near the shore, are the ruined walls of a Portuguese watch-tower. On rising ground about 150 yards east of the watch-tower is the site of the rock-cut elephant, from which the Portuguese christened the island Elephanta, and whose remains are now heaped on the right entrance to the Victoria Gardens in Bombay. This elephant was cut out of an isolated trap boulder and measured about thirteen feet long, seven feet four inches high, eight feet broad, and about twenty feet in girth. Its long tail reached the ground and the belly was

supported by a massive pillar of rock. It originally carried on its back a small elephant about four and half feet long and about one foot broad. Through the brushwood it might easily be taken for a living animal.

About fifty yards to the east of the site of the elephant are the remains of a dwelling, which was built about 1864 for the engineer in charge of the clearing and carrying to Bombay of the lower slopes of the eastern ridge. In these works a large part of the hill was carried away and a bare boulder-strewn flat has been left. The small building with vaulted roof was used to store the gunpowder required for blasting. Somewhere on the west face of the eastern ridge of hills, near the top of the ravine where the hills draw close together, there used to stand a horse, like the elephant carved out of a block of trap. Dr. Fryer (1675) calls it 'the effigies of an horse stuck up to the belly in the earth.' Ovington (1690) describes it more fully, though probably less accurately as 'so lively, with such a colour and carriage, and the shape finished with that exactness that many have fancied it at a distance a living animal rather than only a bare representation.' In 1712 Captain Pyke calls it Alexander's Horse and gives a drawing of it, a stiff zebra-like animal the belly and legs not cut out of the rock. Hamilton (1720) thought it not so well shaped as the elephant. It seems to have disappeared during the next fifty years, as neither Du Perron (1760) nor Niebuhr (1764) notices it. In 1813 Mr. Erskine searched for the horse but found no trace. ... *(pp. 60, 61, 62, 64-65, 80-81, 83-84, 88-89, 90, 91-93)*

Campbell summarises the observations of several writers made on the colossal elephant sculpture that once stood on the island, but now lies near the entrance to the Veermata Jijabai Bhonsle Udyan. While most accounts claim that the elephant disintegrated, it is rumoured that the British wanted to take the sculpture back to England. When they were attempting to lift the elephant, a cable carrying it came loose and the massive sculpture came crashing down. The remains were assembled and subsequently put together.

Garcia D'Orta (1534) calls the island the island of the elephant, but does not make any distinct mention of the elephant. Dom João de Castro (1539) notices the stone elephant in the west, lifelike in colour, size, and features. Linschoten (1578) does not notice it. De Couto (1603) mentions it as the great stone elephant which gave its name to the island. Fryer (1675) calls it a 'monstrous elephant cut out of the main rock bearing a young one on its back.' Ovington (1689) notices 'the statue of an elephant cut in stone in equal proportions to one of those creatures in his full growth.' Its workmanship he calls admirable. In 1712 Captain Pyke made a drawing of the elephant showing a fissure nearly as high as the neck. In 1720 Hamilton found it so like a living animal that at a distance of 200 yards a sharp eye might be deceived. Fifty years later (1760) Du Perron described the elephant as of life size, cut out of black rock, and apparently carrying a young one on its back. In 1764 Niebuhr noticed that it was split and likely to fall in pieces.

It was mentioned by Forbes about 1774 and ten years later was described by Dr. Hunter as twelve feet long and eight high, the trunk pretty well cut and rolled in a spire; the legs shapeless masses out of proportion too large. A massy tail reached to the ground and the hind part of the body was supported by a pillar. It is mentioned by Goldingham (1795) 'as an elephant of black stone large as life.' In 1813 Mr. Erskine and Captain Basil Hall described it as poorly sculptured, though at a distance seen through brushwood it might easily be mistaken for a real elephant. Its length from the head to the root of the tail was thirteen feet two inches and its height at the head seven feet four inches; circumference at the height of the shoulders thirty-five feet five inches, circumference round the four legs thirty-two feet; breadth of the back eight feet; girth of the body twenty feet; length of the leg five feet six inches; circumference of the legs from six feet three inches to seven feet seven inches; length of the supporter two feet two inches; length of the tail seven feet nine inches; length of the trunk seven feet ten inches and remains of the right tusk eleven inches. In September 1814 the head and neck dropped off, and shortly after the body sank to the earth. In 1825 Bishop Heber found it 'much dilapidated by the weather.' In 1835 the trunk and head were separated from the body, and lay broken and prostrate on the ground. In 1859 it was a shapeless mass of rock. In 1863 an attempt was made to move it to England, but, while lifting it, the chains of the crane gave way, the rock got broken, and what remained was removed in 1864 to the right hand entrance of the Victoria Gardens at Byculla, where it lies an almost shapeless mass of rock, though the rolled trunk is distinctly visible. The small elephant on its back is mentioned by Fryer (1675) and Pyke (1712) whose drawing shows the trunk and tusks. It is noticed by Du Perron in 1760. Four years later it appears to have been much defaced, as (1764) Niebuhr describes the large elephant as having on its back something which age had so much worn that it was impossible to make out what it was. Dr. Hunter (1784) found something on the back but with no traces of having been a small elephant. In 1814 Mr. Erskine and Captain Basil Hall mounted the back of the elephant and found distinct marks of four paws, showing that the animal was four feet seven inches long by one foot two inches broad. *(p. 92n. 1)*

HISTORICAL AND DESCRIPTIVE GUIDE TO THE ROCK-CUT CAVES OF ELEPHANTA
by Richard Harris

Richard Harris draws similarities between the sculptures at Elephanta and Egypt in this 1905 publication on Elephanta.

Many tourists visiting these caves remark on the resemblance to the Egyptian style of sculpture, specially in the case of the right hand Doorkeeper at the south door of the Linga Chapel, where the similarity is distinctly perceptible from the waist upwards. One gentleman in particular to manifest the possibility of the Egyptian workmanship, illustrated how he had found the lotus flower (which is *purely* an Indian flower) carved on several sculptures in Egypt, and as these are known to be over 5,000 years in existence, it can be regarded as evidence sufficient to establish the fact of the Egyptians having visited India before that period to have been able to obtain this flower. If the carving was not done by them exactly at, or about that period, their services may have been utilized at some subsequent date, and this possibility may strengthen the greater antiquity of the caves, bringing us nearer the native theory of the 4,000 years. *(p. 12)*

Guardian figure of the linga *shrine in the main cave.*

A GUIDE TO ELEPHANTA by Hirananda Sastri

Hirananda Sastri was an epigraphist with the British government. In his 1934 book on Elephanta, he gives historical and iconographical accounts of the caves.

The sculptures of Elephanta are exclusively Brahmanical in origin and supply us with beautiful specimens of early mediæval Hindu art. There can be no two opinions regarding the decorative side, which is unreservedly praised by all. Opinions differ, however, regarding the formative side or the figure sculpture. The critic, not conversant with Hindu mythology and its underlying idealism, may not be able to fully appreciate the Brahmanical sculpture, especially when it is 'supernatural'. But, one familiar with Hinduism cannot but admire and appreciate the beauty and artistic skill of the workmanship. The late Dr. Vincent Smith, in whom 'mediæval sculpture' seems to have 'aroused a feeling of repulsion', had to admit that it had 'undeniable merits'. One might unhesitatingly say with him that the works of the artists "frequently display high technical skill, great mastery over intractable material, and in the larger compositions, especially those of the western caves, bold imagination and a knowledge of the effects of light and shade. The best specimens of the ascetic type are endowed with serene dignity and convey the impression of perfect repose with extraordinary skill. ...

... The *Thana District Gazetteer* speaks of two inscribed copper-plates also, which were found 'in clearing earth in the north-east corner of the Island and are believed to have been in England in the possession of one Mr. Harold Smith, a contractor, who took them there about 1865 A.D.' No information is available as to their contents and the place where they are now preserved. ...

There are several local traditions or folk-tales connected with the origin of these excavations, but they are of little or no historical value. One of them connects the excavations with the five Pándava heroes of the Mahābhārata; another, with the mythical Asura king Bāna and his beautiful daughter Ushā, while the third ascribes them to Alexander the Great! ...

From the time it was occupied by the British in 1774, a small garrison was maintained on the Island for many years in connection with the harbour defences and the caves were then under the military authorities. In 1875, King Edward VII, then Prince of Wales, was entertained here at a banquet. From 1890 the Public Works Department began to look after the monuments and take steps to arrest ... further decay. Many of the pillars, which were in a parlous condition, were strengthened and repaired, though a good deal of what was desirable from an archæological point of view could not be accomplished. In 1909, the monuments of the Island were declared "Protected" under the Ancient Monuments Preservation Act. Since then they are being conserved ... by the Indian Archæological Department.
(pp. iv-v, 5-6, 12)

PROTECTING THE SITE

by Tasneem Mehta
Convenor, INTACH, Greater Mumbai Chapter

The Indian National Trust for Art and Cultural Heritage (INTACH) was founded in 1984 by the late prime minister Indira Gandhi and has its headquarters in New Delhi. The country's foremost non-governmental, non-profit organisation, it seeks to conserve and promote India's natural and cultural heritage. As a membership-based institution, it encourages public participation in its activities. Since 1997, the Greater Mumbai Chapter of INTACH has been working towards protecting Elephanta island and its caves.

India has for the longest time neglected its heritage and its great monuments, almost afraid, it would seem, to cherish their magnificence. Historians offer many reasons for this neglect: poverty, lack of education, a fear of being seen as elitist and a view of the world that tolerates decay as part of the cycle of life. However, expectations that the tourism industry will be the largest growth sector in the new millennium are changing attitudes. Indians are beginning to recognise that their monuments are potential economic assets and their great cultural heritage deserves care and attention.

The caves of Elephanta, among the most spectacular monuments in India, have unfortunately not received the attention they deserve. This is despite UNESCO having declared these as a World Heritage Site in 1987. Over the years, Elephanta has been exposed to several perils, many of which have had a direct impact on the caves.

Isolated by a body of water, the island faces various environmental hazards due to its location in the middle of Mumbai harbour, which is the country's busiest port. Underwater blasting and pollution caused by port activities are among the many problems threatening Elephanta. Oil spills and the emptying of bilge-water by ships not only pollute the sea, but also impact the mangroves along the shore, destroying the natural ecosystem. Flotsam from ship-breaking activities at Darukhana, situated on the periphery of Mumbai harbour, also finds its way to the island, contaminating the coastline and seriously damaging the mangroves. Apart from this, the Thane Creek area, with Elephanta located at its mouth, is surrounded by oil and chemical industries, making it extremely polluted and lifeless. The Jawaharlal Nehru Port Trust (JNPT), the largest container port in the country, located 500 m from Elephanta island, is proposing to establish a hazardous chemical storage facility.

Apart from these human-generated hazards, the island is also exposed to natural calamities. It is located on a tectonic fault line and is increasingly susceptible to earthquakes with an intensity of 6 to 7 on the Richter scale.

Development on Elephanta – once considered the equivalent of Mount Kailasa, the abode of Shiva, where pilgrims went to meditate and purify themselves – has consisted of beer bars, disorganised hawkers and toy trains. The island has a shortage of potable water and has no regular electric supply – a bit of an ignominy when just across the waters its inhabitants look out at the glittering lights of Mumbai. Besides this, education and health facilities for the island community are inadequate and garbage disposal is a serious problem. While numerous government agencies are actively involved with the administration of Elephanta, there has been very little co-ordination between them, proving to be detrimental to the island's development.

INTACH, Greater Mumbai Chapter, has ventured into this warren of problems in the hope that it could act as a catalyst by working with the government and the local people to promote the right kind of development and help unravel some of the problems that bedevil both the monument and the island of Elephanta. It has been INTACH's endeavour to bring together all the stakeholders involved and to implement planned development strategies to ensure that the site receives the attention it deserves.

INTACH's Elephanta Project began in 1997 with the aim of protecting and raising awareness about the site. Since then the organisation has held a series of seminars and workshops, as well as a unique and very successful benefit event to raise funds for its work on the island. INTACH's objective has been to address the broad issues related to the management of world heritage sites, and ensure that the principles of conservation of the site and cultural tourism, as enshrined in the UNESCO

charters, are followed appropriately. It has also been pivotal in the establishment of the high-powered Statutory Apex Committee, a body appointed by Maharashtra's chief minister, responsible for monitoring the development on Elephanta. This committee functions under the aegis of the Mumbai Metropolitan Regional Development Authority (MMRDA). It is for the first time in India that such a high-powered statutory committee has been set up to manage a World Heritage Site.

UNESCO requires that all World Heritage Sites should have a Visitor Management Plan. In 1998, INTACH together with the Archaeological Survey of India (ASI), prepared such a plan. This was the prelude to the Comprehensive Master Plan which is presently being put together by INTACH, in consultation with the MMRDA Apex Committee. The Visitor Management Plan, which was

Head of Vishnu in the Site Museum at Elephanta.

implemented by the ASI in close association with INTACH, received funding from UNESCO. As part of the plan, the hundred-year-old ASI custodian's cottage at Elephanta was restored and in 1999 a Site Museum was established there. The museum showcases the history and development of cave architecture and rock-cut sculpture in Mumbai as well as in other parts of Maharashtra.

The successful implementation of development objectives necessitates an understanding of the human and political dynamics on the island. Recognising the need to involve the community of the island in any development effort that focuses on the heritage site, INTACH understood that successful tourism plans must include policies for community development, infrastructure, environment and education, if the needs for heritage conservation and sustainable tourism are to be met. INTACH has succeeded in providing an opportunity for the various stakeholders of the island to share a common platform and discuss in a transparent manner issues related to the site. These issues range from the environment stresses faced by the caves, development on the island, tourism, conservation, as well as micro-level livelihood matters relevant to the island dwellers.

The maintenance and conservation of the caves is the responsibility of the ASI. Water seepage in the caves is a serious problem that the ASI has to continually cope with. In addition, it has had to restore several pillars and lintels in the caves to prevent them

A computer-generated rendering of the proposed improvements to the jetty area at Elephanta.

from collapsing. However, the use of cement in its restoration works has created considerable controversy. It is known that cement could have a damaging impact on the stone. In the past, this dispute had caused the ASI to stop its work for a few years.

In an effort to address the livelihood concerns of the inhabitants of the island, INTACH is working with Project Mainstream and Gharda Foundation, both non-governmental organisations that function under the umbrella of the Rotary Club of Bombay, to assist the local community with employment generation opportunities. Many training programmes to enhance retail and management skills of the entrepreneurs on the island, as well as a programme to train women in income-generating activities have been conducted. A women's self-help association and a micro-credit group has been established for the benefit of the people of the island. Enhanced education facilities, establishment of a school for young children and training of teachers has received an enthusiastic response from the island community.

Another problem that plagues the island is the growing population of monkeys. These primates are a serious threat for both the visitors and the local people of the island and INTACH is exploring ways to control their population with the help of the Forest Department and animal welfare NGOs.

As there is no organised conservancy programme, plastic and other waste materials degrade the natural and spiritual beauty of this unique site. The MMRDA Apex Committee is actively looking for solutions to this problem. Attempts to address the issue of chronic water shortage and an inefficient electric supply from diesel generators have resulted in the recent establishment of three new high-efficiency generators on the island and the desilting of five old wells. However, these are temporary measures as the Apex Committee is investigating the feasibility of setting up a permanent solar or hybrid energy supply. INTACH is also in the process of putting together an integrated natural resources development plan for the island, which includes methods to capture rainwater for forest and ground water regeneration, and a proposal for rooftop rainwater harvesting for the villages. As part of a larger eco-tourism plan, there is also a scheme for the regeneration of the mangroves and the establishment of a marine bird sanctuary.

Various proposals for appropriate signage, street furniture and shelters, development control regulations, improvement of the roads and the access path to the site, apart from other infrastructure especially regarding health, education and community facilities, have been included as part of the Comprehensive Master Plan.

Given the value of this site and the unprecedented pressures it is subject to, the need to declare the entire island an environmentally sensitive zone has been stressed time and again. As Elephanta is declared a World Heritage Site, under an international protocol, the central government is in a position to legislate on the subject, and efforts are being made to ensure that this is done at the earliest.

VISITING ELEPHANTA

BOAT SERVICE

A daily boat service operates between the Gateway of India and Elephanta. Boats leave the Gateway every half hour from 9 am to 2:30 pm and the journey lasts an hour.

At Elephanta, the boats leave for the Gateway every half hour starting from 10 am. The last boat back to Mumbai leaves at 5:30 pm.

Boat tickets are available at the counter of Gateway Elephanta Jal Vahathuk Sanstha, situated at the end of Apollo Bunder road near Gateway of India. Tickets can also be purchased on the boat itself. Private boats can be booked from Gateway Elephanta Jal Vahathuk Sanstha.

TICKETS
Deluxe:

Adults	Rs 85
Children (below 7 years)	Rs 55

Economy:

Adults	Rs 65
Children (below 7 years)	Rs 40

CATAMARAN SERVICE

Gateway Elephanta Pleasure Tour and Travels runs a daily catamaran, which leaves from the Gateway at 10 am and returns at 2 pm. An English-speaking guide accompanies the group and the journey takes 40 minutes. Tickets can be bought at the Gateway Elephanta Jal Vahathuk Sanstha counter.

TICKETS

Adults	Rs 90
Children (below 7 years)	Rs 50

ELEPHANTA CAVES

The caves are open from 10 am to 5 pm on all days except Mondays.

TICKETS

Indians	Rs 10
Foreigners	US$ 5

SITE MUSEUM

The Site Museum on the island is located opposite the ticket counter, near the entrance to the main cave. The ticket fee for the caves includes a visit to the museum.

RESTAURANTS

The main restaurant on the island is run by the Maharashtra Tourism Development Corporation (MTDC). There are also many smaller restaurants. MTDC has two rooms which can be rented only during the day as overnight stay on Elephanta is not permitted.

ELEPHANTA FESTIVAL

This festival is organised once a year by the MTDC, usually in the month of February. It includes music and dance performances near the caves by eminent Indian artists.

A WORD OF CAUTION

The island is populated by numerous monkeys, and though normally docile, they can be aggravated if teased or hurt. It is advisable to avoid drinking or eating in their presence.

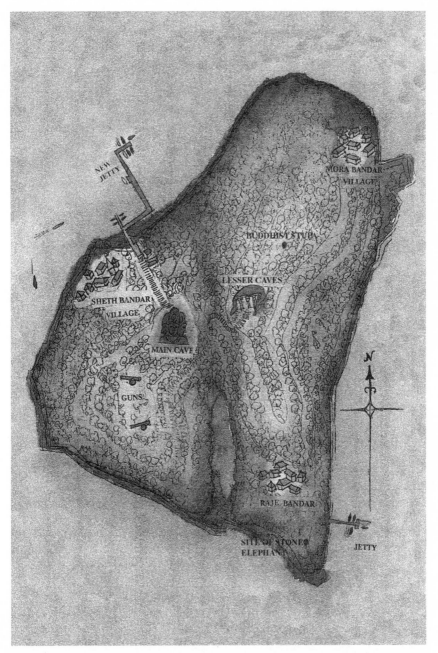

A popular tourist map of Elephanta island indicating the location of the caves and other important landmarks.

GLOSSARY

Aghora-Bhairava: angry aspect of Shiva
Airavata: elephant mount of Indra
Andhaka: demon speared by Shiva
Andhakasuravadha: Shiva impaling Andhaka
Ardhanarishvara: androgynous form of Shiva
Bhagiratha: sage who compelled Shiva to ask Ganga to descend to the earth
Bhringi: emaciated attendant of Shiva
Bodhisattva: Buddhist saviour
Brahma: first god of Hindu trinity, the Creator
chaitya: Buddhist congregational hall
chakra: disc weapon of Vishnu·
Chandra: moon god
charmukha: four-faced
chauri: fly-whisk
darshana: an auspicious view
dvarapala: guardian figure
ekamukha: one-faced
gana: impish dwarf associated with Shiva
gandharva: celestial being
Ganesha: elephant-headed Hindu god
Ganga: goddess who became river Ganga
Gangadhara: Shiva bearing Ganga
Garuda: eagle mount of Vishnu
Himavant: god of Himalayas, father of Parvati
Hiranyakashipu: demon who was disembowelled by Vishnu
Indra: warrior god of the heavens
jata: matted hair
Jyeshtha: Shiva as protector
Kalyanasundara: marriage of Shiva and Parvati
Kama: god of love
Kapila: the great ascetic
Karttikeya: asectic warrior god, son of Parvati and Shiva
Lakshmi: goddess of wealth
Lakulisha: Shiva holding the club; founder of the Pashupata sect
lalita: forceful posture with one hand thrown across the chest
linga: phallic emblem of Shiva
Mahadeva, Maheshvara: the Great Lord, epithets of Shiva

Mahishasuramardini: goddess Durga killing Mahisha, the buffalo demon
makara: crocodile-like aquatic monster
mandapa: columned hall
Markandeya: youthful devotee of Shiva
matrika: mother goddess
moksha: ultimate liberation of the soul
Mount Kailasa: mountain home of Shiva
mudra: symbolic hand gesture
naga: serpent
Nandi: bull mount of Shiva
Narasimha: man-lion incarnation of Vishnu
Nataraja: Shiva as Lord of Dance
Nila: demon who assumed an elephant form
Nrityashastra: ancient Sanskrit text on dance
panchamukha: five-faced
Parvati: consort of Shiva
Pashupata: sect of Shaivas
prana: the breath of life
pradakshina: circumambulation
Puranas: collections of mythological stories
Ramayana: major Hindu epic, story of Rama
Ravana: demon king of Lanka
Rudra: Shiva as destroyer
Sadashiva: Eternal Shiva, the god in his cosmic form with multiple heads
Sadyojata-Nandin: Shiva's unseen fourth face
Shaiva: pertaining to the cult of Shiva
Shiva: third god of Hindu trinity, who is both creative and destructive
Shivaratri: a festival celebrating Shiva
Sita: consort of the god Rama
tandava: destructive dance of Shiva
Tatpurusha-Mahadeva: central face of Shiva
torana: gateway or portal
Umamaheshvara: Shiva gambling with Parvati
Vamadeva-Uma: female aspect of Shiva as creator
Varaha: boar-headed incarnation of Vishnu
Varuna: god of the oceans
vihara: Buddhist monastery
Vishnu: second god of Hindu trinity, the Preserver
Yogishvara: Lord of Yogis, Shiva as a yogi
yuga: four ages of the world

*Tiger Gate
Elephanta Cave.
Bombay.*

There are many of these besides. Even they are beautifully carved; minute.

Supplied by Thacker & Co., Ld., Bombay. Wanowrie Lines, Poona.   Elephanta Caves. Bombay.   July 25. 1904 Made in Saxony

Hoping you are all right again & having a good time up north — Jim.

*Early 20th-century
postcards of Elephanta.*

SELECT BIBLIOGRAPHY

BERKSON, CARMEL, WENDY DONIGER O'FLAHERTY AND GEORGE MICHELL. *Elephanta: The Cave of Shiva*. Princeton University Press, 1983

BURGESS, JAMES. *Report on the Elura Cave Temples and the Brahmanical and Jaina Temples in Western India*. London: Trübuer and Co, 1883

CAMPBELL, JAMES M. "Thana: Places of Interest". *Gazetteer of the Bombay Presidency*. Vol. XIV. Bombay: Government Central Press, 1882

CHANDRA, PRAMOD. *A Guide to the Elephanta Caves*. Bombay: Bhulabhai Memorial Institute, 1957

COLLINS, CHARLES W. *The Iconography and Ritual of Siva at Elephanta*. Rochester: State University of New York Press, 1988

ERSKINE, WILLIAM. "Account of the Cave-Temple of Elephanta with a Plan and Drawings of the Principal Figures". *Transactions of the Literary Society of Bombay*. Vol. I. London: John Murray, 1819

FORBES, JAMES. *Oriental Memoirs*. Vol. I. London: White, Cochrane, and Co Horace's Head, 1813

FRYER, JOHN. *A New Account of East-India and Persia in Eight Letters being Nine Years Travels*. London: R I Chiswell, 1698

HARRIS, RICHARD. *Historical and Descriptive Guide to the Rock-cut Caves of Elephanta*. Bombay: Methodist E Publishing House, 1905

HEBER, REGINALD. *Narrative of a Journey through the Upper Provinces of India from Calcutta to Bombay, 1824-1825*. Vol. III. 3rd ed. London: John Murray, 1828

KHANDALAVALA, KARL. *The Island Shrine of Elephanta*. Hyderabad, 1990

KRAMRISCH, STELLA. "The Great Cave Temple of Siva on the Island of Elephanta". *The Presence of Siva*. Princeton University Press, 1981

MITTER, PARTHA. *Much Maligned Monsters: A History of European Reaction to Indian Art*. Oxford University Press, 1977

OUSELEY, SIR WILLIAM. *Travels in Various Countries of the East*. Vol. I. London: Rodwell and Martin, 1819

OVINGTON, J A. *A Voyage to Suratt in the Year 1689*. Edited with an introduction by J P Guha. New Delhi: Associated Publishing House, 1976

SASTRI, HIRANANDA. *A Guide to Elephanta*. Delhi: Manager of Publications, 1934

SPINK, WALTER M. "The Great Cave at Elephanta: A Study of Sources". *Essays on Gupta Culture*. Edited by Bardwell L Smith. Delhi: South Asia Books, 1983

VALENTIA, VISCOUNT GEORGE. *Voyages and Travels to India, Ceylon, the Red Sea, Abyssinia, and Egypt*. Vol. II. London: William Miller, 1809

WILSON, JOHN. *Lecture on the Religious Excavations of Western India, Buddhist, Brahmanical, and Jaina, including the Details of those of Elephanta and Karla*. Bombay: Education Society's Press, 1875

ILLUSTRATIONS *A listing of archival material*

CREDITS

ISBN 81-7508-327-1

TEXT
© 2002 George Michell

PHOTOGRAPHY
© 2002 Bharath Ramamrutham
unless otherwise indicated

PUBLISHED BY
India Book House Pvt Ltd
412 Tulsiani Chambers
Nariman Point, Mumbai 400 021, India
Tel 91 22 284 0165   Fax 91 22 283 5099
E-mail ibhpub@vsnl.com